Annapolis: The Guidebook

1999

Edited by Katie Moose

Illustrations by Ginger Doyel

Conduit Press
Annapolis, Maryland

This book is dedicated to George Moose and Stanley and Loretta Larrimore who taught the author the appreciation and beauty of Annapolis and more particularly the Chesapeake Bay region. And to Lucinda Holmes for being the most wonderful, loving and thoughtful daughter.

Copyright ©1999 Conduit Press

Published by the Conduit Press, 111 Conduit Street, Annapolis, Maryland 21401.

Library of Congress Cataloging-in-Publication Data

Printed and Bound by Victor Graphics, Inc., Baltimore, Maryland, USA

ISBN: 0-9666610-0-1

Table of Contents

Illustrations

Introduction

History and sailing abound in Annapolis. In fact Annapolis will celebrate its 350th anniversary in 1999. Annapolis was the second capital of Maryland, but the capital of the colonies during the Revolutionary War. The Articles of Confederation were written by Thomas Stone, one of the three signers of the Declaration of Independence from Annapolis. George Washington resigned his commission in the Continental Army here in 1783. The Treaty of Paris was signed 1784 signaling the end of the Revolution. In addition St. John's College is the third oldest in the U.S. founded 1696, after Harvard and William and Mary.

This sailing capital of the world hosts not only some of the grandest yachts, but once skipjacks, schooners, bugeyes, log canoes and the Trumpy yachts. In 1998 Annapolis was a stop and departure point for the Whitbread Around the World Race. It was appropriate the Naval Academy should be founded here in 1845.

Annapolis lies at the convergence of the Chesapeake Bay (from the Algonquin Indian name "Chesepiook" which can mean "The great shellfish bay", "big river at", "mother of waters", "great salty bay", or "on the big bay") and the Severn River. To the north lies the Bay Bridge and beyond that Baltimore. To the south the Chesapeake flows to the Atlantic. Along the way are numerous creeks and rivers, often with lovely places to tie up or moor for an overnight or longer.

Though Annapolis is a capital and city life is relaxed, the city retains the formalness of a southern town. Politicians keep up a busy schedule January to April at the State House; sailors sail year round; and a host of events keep Annapolitans and visitors on their toes. Midshipmen from the Naval Academy wander in uniforms, while others meander in shorts or something comfortable. Businessmen wear anything from suits to shorts. Somehow, even with this fast paced world, there is time to enjoy the May baskets on the doors, listen to good music, walk along the seawall at the Naval Academy, or enjoy a sunset sail. Annapolis is truly a haven for those seeking history, magnificent architecture and the Bay.

1

Chapter 1

Informative Tips about Annapolis

Calendar of Events

January, February
- Friday evening concerts at the Naval Academy, or events at the Maryland Center for Creative Arts.
- Sunday afternoons there are frostbite races sponsored by several yacht clubs and sailing associations.

March
- St. Patrick's Day – parades and other activities in local pubs
- Caritas Society Flower and Garden Show
- Marlborough Hunt Races. Roedown Farm, Davidsonville. 410-798-5040

May
- 1- May Basket Competition - doors decorated with baskets of flowers
- 1st Sunday in May - Chesapeake Bay Bridge Walk.
- Annapolis Waterfront Arts Festival. 410-268-8828
- United States Naval Academy Commissioning Week

June
- Jazzfest. St. John's College. Admission. 410-647-4449
- Mid-Atlantic Wine Festival. Anne Arundel Fair Grounds. 410-280-3306
- Annapolis to Newport Race: Annapolis to Bermuda Race
- Leukemia Cup Race

July
- Induction Day for new Midshipmen at Naval Academy
- Independence Day celebrations
- Tuesday night concerts on City Dock
- Thursday night concerts at Naval Academy

3

August
- Annual Governor's Cup Race
- Crab Feast. Navy-Marine Corps Stadium. 410-267-9330

September
- Maryland Renaissance Fair. Week-ends and Labor Day through October. Crownsville Road. Admission. 410-266-7304
- Labor Day Parade
- Maryland Seafood Festival. Sandy Point State Park. 410-268-7682
- Hospice Cup Regatta 410-216-6400
- Anne Arundel County Fair. Fairgrounds. 410-923-3400

October
- Chesapeake Appreciation Day. Sandy Point State Park . 410-268-7722
- U.S. Sailboat Show. City Dock. Admission. 410-268-8828
- U.S. Powerboat Show. City Dock. Admission 410-268-8828
- Anne Arundel Scottish Highland Games. Fairgrounds. 410-849-2849

November
- Candlelight Tour. Sponsored by Historic Annapolis Foundation. Admission. 410-544-1363
- Lights on the Bay. Sponsored by Anne Arundel Medical Center. Every evening 5-11PM. Sandy Point State Park. Admission. 410-267-1373
- Friday after Thanksgiving. Arrival of Santa Claus. City Dock
- Waterfowl Festival in Easton.

December
- Deck the Halls. Houses and buildings decorated for holidays
- State House by Candlelight Tour. 410-974-2400
- Doll House Exhibit. Barge House Museum. Eastport. 410-268-2454
- Midnight Madness. Shops open till midnight (one night only, date varies)
- Annapolis Holiday and Yacht Tour. 410-280-0445
- Annual Eastport Yacht Club Festival of Lights. Boat Parade. Spa Creek and Ego Alley. 410-263-0415
- New Year's Eve First Night Annapolis. Admission. 410-787-2717

January-April   Maryland Legislature meets at the State House

4

Directions to Annapolis

Annapolis, located in Anne Arundel County, is less than one hour from Washington and Baltimore, off Route 50 before the Bay Bridge.

Recommended Parking

Please park at the Navy Marine Corps Stadium off Rowe Blvd. Take the shuttle bus to town and tourist destinations. Downtown garages fill quickly.
Hillman Garage - Duke of Gloucester Street
Gott's Court Garage. Whitman Garage. Both off Calvert Street
Street Parking - permitted 2 hours on week days, 3 hours on week-ends
Meters- usually for ½-1 hour

Public Rest Rooms

Harbor Master's Building. City Dock
Conference and Visitor's Bureau. 26 West Street

Airports

Baltimore-Washington International.
Reagan National
Washington Dulles International

Buses

Annapolis Transit. 410-263-7964
Mass Transit Authority (Annapolis, Baltimore, Washington). 410-539-5000

Taxis/Limousine Service

Reliable Cab. 410-268-4714
A-A1st Class Limousine.410-268-0009
Annapolis Cab Company.410-268-0022
Airport Cabs.410-859-1100
Arundel 7Colonial Cab.410-263-2555
Blue Star/Crown Diamond.410-263-4444

Blue Star/Crown Diamond.410-263-4444
Capitol City Cab.410-267-0000
Yellow Checker Cab.410-268-3737

Auto Rentals

Hertz . 800-654-3131
Sears. 2002 West Street. 410-266-8233
Budget. 2002 West Street. 410-266-5030
Discount Rent-A-Car. 1032 West Street. 410-268-5955
Enterprise Rent-A-Car. 1023 Spa Road. 410-268-7751
Avis. 800-831-2847
Alamo. 800-327-9633

Towing

Darden's. 410-269-1046

Motor Vehicle Department

If you are moving to the state you must obtain a driver's license and register your car within 30 days of your move. Downtown residents of Annapolis need a parking permit. The MVA is located at 160 Harry S. Truman Parkway.

Information

Remember all telephone numbers in Maryland are 10 digit. You must dial 410 first.
Greater Annapolis Chamber of Commerce. 1 Annapolis Street. 410-268-7676
Conference and Visitors Bureau. 26 West Street. 410-280-0445
City Hall. 160 Duke of Gloucester Street. 410-263-1123. The Mayor and Aldermen are elected for four year terms. The mayor can run for two consecutive terms, the aldermen indefinitely.
Historic Annapolis Foundation Welcome Center and Museum Store. 77 Main Street. 410-268-5576
Arundel Trade Council. 1460 Ritchie Highway, Arnold. 410-757-6709
Marine Trades Association of Maryland. PO Box 3148. 410-269-0741

Important Telephone Numbers

Emergency Number 911
Anne Arundel Medical Center. Franklin and Cathedral Streets. 410-267-1000
Annapolis Police 410-268-9000
Drug Hotline 800-752-DRUG
Alcoholic Anonymous 800-492-0209
Youth Crisis Hotline 800-422-0009
Poison Center 800-492-2414
Annapolis Harbor Master 410-263-7973
Coast Guard Station, Annapolis 410-267-8108
Annapolis Fire Department 410-263-7975
EMS Division 410-263-7978
Public Works Department 410-263-7049
Transportation Department 410-263-7964
Public Information and Tourism 410-263-7940
Visitor Information Booth 410-268-TOUR

Sightseeing and Harbor Tours

Annapolis Walkabout. 410-263-8253
Chesapeake Marine Tours. City Dock. 410-268-7600
Historic Annapolis Foundation Tours. 26 West Street. 410-263-5533
Naval Academy Tour Guide Service. Visitors Center. Gate 1. 410-293-3363
Three Centuries Tours. 48 Maryland Avenue. 410-263-5401
Discover Annapolis Tours. Departs from 26 West Street. 410-626-6000
Annapolis Gardening School and Tours. 410-263-6041
Historic Annapolis African-American Heritage Walking Tour. 410-268-5576
Schooner "Woodwind". Marriott Harborfront Hotel. 410-263-7837

Magazines

Inside Annapolis. 519 Burnside Street. 410-263-6300
Spin Sheet. 301 Fourth Street. 410-216-9309
Chesapeake Life. PO Box 3323 410-280-2777
Chesapeake Bay. 1819 Bay Ridge Avenue. 410-263-2662

Newspapers

The Capital. 2000 Capital Drive. 410-268-5000
Washington Post. 1150 15th Street, NW, Washington, DC. 202-334-6000
The Washington Times. 3600 New York Avenue, NE, Washington, DC. 202-269-3419
Baltimore Sun. 501 N. Calvert Street, Baltimore. 800-829-8000
The Publick Enterprise. 410-268-3527

Radio Stations

WNAV Radio (1430 AM)

Special Events and Places

Maryland Hall for the Creative Arts. 801 Chase Street. 410-263-5544
Naval Academy. 410-293-2439
St. John's College. 410-263-2371
Mitchell Gallery, St. John's College. 410-263-2371
Annapolis Symphony. 410-263-0907
Annapolis Chorale   410-263-1906
Annapolis Waterfront Arts Festival. 410-268-8828
Annapolis Summer Garden Theatre. 143 Compromise Street. 410-268-9212
Colonial Players. 108 East Street. 410-268-7373
Maryland Center for the Creative Arts. 801 Chase Street. 410-263-1906
Ballet Theatre of Annapolis. Maryland Hall for the Creative Arts. 410-543-6353

Music

Maryland Center for the Creative Arts. 801 Chase Street. 410-263-1906
Chesapeake Music Hall. Busch's Frontage Road. 410-626-7515
U.S. Naval Academy Concerts. 410-293-2439
City Dock. Concerts during summer

Movie Theaters

Annapolis Harbour Center. 410-224-1145
Eastport Cinemas. 410-224-1145
Annapolis Mall. 410-224-1145

8

Sailing

Please see chapter on Yachting

Golf

Annapolis Golf Club. 2638 Carrollton Road. Semi-private. 410-263-6771
Bay Hills Golf Club. 545 Bay Hills Drive, Arnold. Semi-private. 410-974-0669
Dwight D. Eisenhower Golf Club. Generals Highway, Crownsville. Public. 410-222-7922
Severna Park Golf Center. 1257 Ritchie Highway, Arnold. Public. 410-647-8618
South River Golf Links. Routes 2 and 214, Edgewater. Public. 410-798-5865

Favorite Fishing Spots

Old Severn River Bridge

Biking and Hiking

Quiet Waters Park. Hillsmere Drive
The B&A Trail on old railroad tracks goes 13.3 miles from Annapolis to Glen Burnie

Swimming

The best swimming is on the ocean side, not Bay. In the Bay beware of nettles, otherwise known as medusa jellyfish that cause a burning sensation. This should only last a few minutes. Also during the summer mosquitoes and flies do show up at the beaches.
Sandy Point Park
Truxtun Park Pool
Bay Ridge - private
Arundel Olympic Swim Center. Riva Road. 410-222-7933

Tennis

Truxtun Park. Truxtun Road

Parks

Anne Arundel Recreation and Parks. 410-222-7317
Quiet Waters. Hillsmere Drive – picnic, hiking/bicycle trails, gardens, playground, ice rink, boat rentals, lectures, concerts
Truxtun Park - ball fields, swimming, tennis, picnic tables, boat ramp
B&A Trail. Old railroad bed from Glen Burnie to Annapolis. 13.3 miles
Helen Avalynne Tawes Garden. Rowe Blvd. Six acre botanical sanctuary
Sandy Point State Park. West end of Bay Bridge off Route 50.
Downs Park. 8311 John Downs Loop. Pasadena. 230 acre park on Chesapeake.
Jug Bay Wetlands Sanctuary. 1361 Wrighton Road. Lothian. 620 acre natural preserve.
Lake Waterford Park. Pasadena Road and B&A Blvd. Pasadena. Lake, picnic area.
Mayo Beach Park. Honeysuckle Drive, Edgewater. On South River. By permit only.

Canoeing and Kayaking

Up and down any of the numerous creeks, rivers and the Chesapeake

Bicycle Rentals/Sales

Bike Doctor. 150 P Jennifer Road. 410-266-7383

Hunting

Hunting is a favorite pastime. Especially popular are duck, Canada geese, dove and deer.

Baseball

Baltimore Orioles - Camden Yards, Baltimore. 410-481-SEAT
Baysox. Route 301, south of route 50. 301-805-6000
Naval Academy. 410-268-6060

Football

Naval Academy. 410-268-6060
Ravens. Baltimore. 410-261-7283
Redskins. 301-276-6050

Schools

Anne Arundel County Public Schools. Riva Road. 410-222-5303
Annapolis Area Christian School. Bestgate Road. Grades 1-12. 410-266-8251
St. Anne's Day School. 3112 Arundel on the Bay Road. Grades nursery-6.
410-263-8650
The Key School. 534 Hillsmere Drive. 1-12. Grades nursery-12. 410-263-9231
Severn School. Severna Park. 410-647-7701
Indian Creek School. Evergreen Road. Crownsville. 410-987-0342
St. Margaret's Day School. 1601 Pleasant Plains Road. 410-757-2333
St. Martin's Lutheran School. 1120 Spa Road. 410-269-1955
St. Andrew's School. 4 Wallace Manor Road, Edgewater. 410-266-0952
St. Mary's School. Duke of Gloucester Street. 410-263-3294

Colleges

U.S. Naval Academy.410-293-1000
St. John's. 410-263-2371
Anne Arundel Community College. Arnold. 410-647-7100

Libraries

Annapolis -1410 West Street. 410-222-1750
Eastport-Annapolis. 269 Hillsmere Drive. 410-222-1770
Naval Academy. This is not often open to the public, but it has beautiful views
of the Severn River, numerous technical books and magazines, plus a lot about
the US Navy.

How to Make it in Annapolis

Dressing the part

Dress is very important in Annapolis. Annapolis is basically a casual town. However because it is the capital of Maryland and a city, appropriate dress is advised. Ladies should not be seen in short shorts, low cut dresses or bathing suits.
Men should not wear tank tops, tee shirts, short shorts, or be bare chested. No bathing suits except at the beach.

The town is oriented toward sailing, and one has to go some distance to find a swimming area, tennis courts or golf course.

Men

Daytime:
Khaki pants or shorts
Polo shirts
Topsiders
No socks
Foul weather gear

Evening Wear: Some restaurants and yacht clubs require coat and tie. For yacht christenings and special events navy blue blazer, tan or white pants, club or regimental tie.

Ladies

Daytime
Khaki, linen or silk pants
Shorts
Polo shirt
Blazers or wool sweaters
Topsiders

Evening Wear: Nice dress - silk or cotton. Silk pants and blouse.

The "In Associations" or Clubs

Historic Annapolis Foundation
Auxiliary of Anne Arundel Medical Center
Junior League of Annapolis
Federated Garden Clubs of America – Four Rivers Garden Club
Annapolis Yacht Club
Leukemia Cup and Hospice Cup yacht races

Where to take your favorite girl or beau

Sunday Brunch	Carrol's Creek
Lunch	McGarvey's
Drinks	McGarvey's or Pusser's
Dinner	Treaty of Paris
Music	Surfside7, Ram's Head or Treaty of Paris
Sightseeing	Walking tour of Annapolis
Drive	The Eastern Shore
Sailing	Anywhere on Bay or creeks

Things to do on a great day

Go sailing
Learn to sail
Watch the sailboats
Girl watch on the harbor
Sit at one of the outdoor cafes and people watch
Take a walking tour of Historic Annapolis
Take a picnic to Quiet Waters Park or Thomas Point
Walk around the Naval Academy, especially along the sea wall

Things to Do on a Rainy Day

Visit the William Paca, Chase-Lloyd, or Hammond-Harwood Houses
Visit the Naval Academy - the Museum and Chapel
Visit the State Capital
Go to the Movies
Sit in a bar, meet new friends and be patient. Just don't get drunk as Maryland
has strict DWI laws.

Things to do for free on a Summer Evening

Tuesday night concerts on City Dock
Thursday night concerts at the Naval Academy
Wednesday night boat races
Friday Night Beer Can Series
Watch the sunset every evening from the Bridge on Spa Creek
Watch the sunset every evening from your own boat

Things to do for Free on a Winter Evening

Friday night concerts at Mitscher Hall, Naval Academy
Curl up in front of a fire with a good book
Hang out at one of the local pubs (you will have to purchase a drink or two, but you'll get some lively conversation)
Listen to some good music

Favorite Pets

Black, yellow and chocolate labradors, and Chesapeakes (Chessies) are favorite pets, and are also used for hunting.

Web Sites

http://www.umcp.umd.edu/Campus/Maps/Annapolis/Welcome.html
http://www.city.net/united_states/maryland/annapolis/

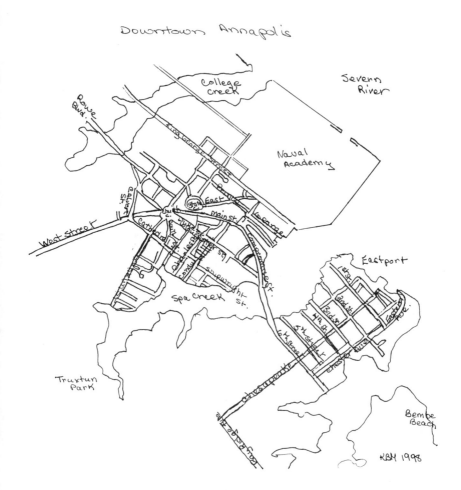

Downtown Annapolis

Chapter 2

Annapolis Walking Tour

Annapolis is a very walkable city. This tour can be completed in about one and a half hours, if you are pressed for time. However, you would miss entering the beautiful museums and homes that are open to the public. Wear comfortable shoes as bricks and cobblestones make walking a little more eyecatching.

As a background note, Annapolis was founded as a Protestant city, as England was ruled by King William at that time. Early names for it were Providence, Severn, Procter's Landing, and Anne Arundel Town. The city was laid out in 1696 by Governor Nicholson around State and Church Circles on 2 hills from which the streets radiate. Today the city sits on 3 peninsulas, four creeks and the Rivers Severn and South, and the Chesapeake Bay.

We start our tour at historic St. Anne's Church on Church Circle. This is the third of three churches which was built on this site, the first in 1692. Maryland had originally been given to Lord Baltimore, a Catholic whose capital was St. Mary's City. Around the circle are the Post Office, Reynolds Tavern, the County Courthouse, the Maryland Inn, and the Governor's Mansion.

The State Capital was first called the Stadt House in deference to the Dutch king William, built in 1697. The building is the oldest continuously used state house in the US. In 1783 Gen. George Washington tendered his resignation here, and in 1784 the Treaty of Paris, formally ending the Revolution was signed here. In 1787 meetings to write the Articles of Confederation were held, later moved to Philadelphia, known as the Philadelphia Constitutional Convention. The Old Senate Chamber with furniture by John Shaw, the USS Maryland Room, the Senate Chamber, Chamber of the House of Delegates, and exhibition rooms are on the main floor. Outside the State House are statues of Roger Brooke Taney, Thurgood Marshall, and Baron De Kalb. On the grounds is the Old Treasury Building.

After going around State Circle turn right onto Maryland Avenue. Here are some lovely shops, art galleries and informal restaurants.

Turn left on Prince George or King George Streets and you will end up at St. John's College founded in 1696. Famous people who attended were Mrs. Washington's grandson George Washington Parke Custis and Francis Scott Key. Courses are taught around 100 great books all of which must be familiar to each professor so that they can teach from any one. Only 400 students are permitted to study here. The Liberty Tree is over 400 years old. Meetings were held under it during the Revolutionary War, and is 1840 some boys almost destroyed it by igniting gunpowder in the trunk.

One of America's early foremost architects was William Buckland who moved to Annapolis in 1772 and designed the Chase-Lloyd House, Gov. Sharpe's house, the Senate Chamber and the Hammond-Harwood House (c 1774). His fine Palladian style set an example for other lovely brick homes located throughout the city, some of which we will pass as we go up Duke of Gloucester Street at the end of our tour. But do look at the fine ones on Maryland Avenue (the Hammond-Harwood House and Chase-Lloyd House) and on Prince George Street the William Paca House and Garden and Brice House.

Stay on College Street and turn right on Hannover. The Peggy Stewart House on the right was once owned by Anthony Stewart, who in 1774 brought a shipload of tea to Annapolis, but was forced to have his own "Tea Party" by beaching his boat on Spa Creek and then burning her.

Come back to the Naval Academy entrance at the end of Maryland Avenue. The Naval Academy Museum is located in Preble Hall just inside the gate, and should not be missed. The Naval Academy, then called the Naval School, was founded in 1845 on land purchased by the Navy Department on Windmill Point from the Dulany family. Originally it had been Fort Severn, composed of 9 acres (The Yard), now 300. The first Superintendent was Franklin Buchanan. The original class had 50 midshipmen and 7 faculty members. Bancroft Hall, a French Renaissance style building of granite, is the largest dormitory in the world, now housing approximately 4000 students. The Chapel, designed like several other campus buildings by New York architect Ernest Flagg, opened in 1904 and the nave was added in 1939. The Prayer Book and Bible belonged to David Farrugut. The crypt houses the body of John Paul Jones, the founder of the US Navy who died in Paris and whose remains were brought here. The statue of Tecumsah is decorated for various football games and other occasions, and is "The God of the passing Grade". If you are visiting around lunch time you might be able to watch the Brigade Noon Formation. The Visitor Center is located at Ricketts Hall and has some very interesting exhibits and Navy items for sale.

Walking away from the Academy on Randall Street at Gate 1 you will come into the center of town, Main Street and the harbor. A Market House has stood here since 1728, the present one built 1858 and restored in 1970 and the City Dock in use since the 1600's. The Historic Annapolis Foundation at 77 Main Street has exhibits and sells items relating to Annapolis. If you're hungry try one of the many restaurants, out door cafes or pick up something from one of the vendors at the Market House. Looking around you will see the historic Middleton Tavern, run in the 1700's by Samuel Middleton, and later used as the federal Customs House. Radiating up the hill are Pinckney, Francis and Cornhill Streets, all very charming.

Walk along the harbor on Compromise Street to the Annapolis Yacht Club and the Spa Creek Bridge. You can look across at Eastport, which is a walk in itself. Turn right on Duke of Gloucester Street. On your left you will pass St. Mary's Church with the historic Charles Carroll House overlooking Spa Creek. On the right are the beautiful Ridout Row homes and the Ridout House. The Annapolis Town Hall is also here.

Turning left on Charles Street you will find lovely brick homes and on the left the Jonas Green House, one of the oldest homes in Annapolis and still occupied by Green descendants. Turn right on Cathedral Street and you will return to West Street.

State Circle Inn

©1998

ginger Doyel

Chapter 3

Lodging

Historic District

Historic Inns of Annapolis 1-800-847-8882
Maryland Inn. Main Street and Church Circle. Large inn dating from 1770's built by merchant Thomas Hyde.
Governor Calvert House. State Circle
Robert Johnson House. State Circle

Annapolis Accomodations. 66 Maryland Avenue. 1-800-715-1000
Bed and Breakfast of Maryland. 800-736-4667
Annapolis Marriott Waterfront. 80 Compromise Street. 410-268-7555
Loews Annapolis Hotel. 126 West Street. 410-263-1299
State House Inn. State Circle. 410-990-0024. Dates from 1820.

Bed and Breakfast

Jonas Greene House. 124 Charles Street. Dates from 1690's. Still owned by descendants of Greene family. (See chapter on Buildings and Places)
Gibson's Lodgings. 110 Prince George Street. 410-268-5555. Three lovely homes in Historic Annapolis. The Patterson House property was assigned to Richard Hill, the first naval officer of the Port of Annapolis in 1681. The present house was built 1760-1786 by Richard MacCubbin.
Georgian House Bed and Breakfast. 170 Duke of Gloucester Street. 410-263-5618. Registered Landmark in Historic District, built 1747 for the Forensic Society
Flag House Inn. 26 Randall Street. 410-280-2721. Victorian B&B in Historic District convenient to Naval Academy
Magnolia House. 220 King George Street. 410-268-3477. Conveniently located in Historic District
William Page Inn. 8 Martin Street. 410-626-1506. William Page was a 19th c English shipbuilder. He never lived in the house, but some of his models can be seen at the Naval Academy Museum in Preble Hall.
Prince George Inn. 232 Prince George Street. 410-626-0009. Victorian built 1884
Hunter House. 154 Prince George Street. 410-626-1268. Federal house dates back to 1870's.
The Blue Heron. 172 Green Street. 410-263-9171. Built 1843

55 East. 55 East Street. 410-295-0202. Italianate home built 1864.
The Gatehouse. 249 Hanover Street. 410-280-0024
Merry Walk. 105 Market Street, 410-268-6233
Duke and Duchess. 151 Duke of Gloucester Street. 410-268-6323
The Corner Cupboard. 30 Randall Street. 410-263-4970
The Doll's House. 161 Green Street. 410-626-2028
Two-O-One. 201 Prince George Street. 410-268-8053
Mary Rob B&B. 243 Prince George Street. 410-268-5438. Victorian Italianate
villa c 1864
Ark and Dove B&B. 149 Prince George Street. 410-268-6277
Charles Inn B&B. 74 Charles Street. 410-268-1451. Built c Civil War
Chez Amis B&B. 85 East Street. 410-263-6631
Coggeshall House. 198 King George Street. 410-263-5068
College House Suites. One College Avenue. 410-263-6124
Green Street Inn. 172 Green Street. 410-263-9171
One-Four-Four B&B. 144 Prince George Street. 410-268-8053
Shaw's Fancy B&B. 161 Green Street. 410-263-0320
Private Pleasure. 60 foot Trumpy yacht.
The Admiral's House. 65 College Street
Eastport House B&B. 101 Severn Avenue. 410-295-9710
The Gloucester House. 151 Duke of Gloucester Street. 410-268-6323
The Inn at Spa Creek. 417 Severn Avenue. Eastport. 410-263-8866
American Heritage B&B. 108 Charles Street. 410-280-1620
The Duchess Inn. 146 Duke of Gloucester Street. 410-267-9262
The Wyatt House Bed & Breakfast. Bay Ridge Avenue, Eastport. 410-626-0771

Special Houses

Keyworth House. 152 Prince George Street. 410-269-5207. In Historic District,
one block from the State Capital. Can be rented for a two night minimum

Hotels and Motels Outside the Historic District

Comfort Inn. 76 Old Mill Bottom Road North. 410-757-8500
Courtyard by Marriott. 2559 Riva Road. 410-266-1555
Days Inn. 2520 Riva Road. 410-224-2800
Holiday Inn. 210 Holiday Court. 410-224-3150
Hampton Inn & Suites. 124 Womack Drive. 410-571-0200
Howard Johnson Motel. Rte. 50/301. 410-757-1600
Wyndham Garden Hotel. Parole and Rte. 50/301. 410-266-3131
Super 8 Motel. 74 Old Mill Bottom Road north. 410-757-2222

Residence Inn by Marriott. 170 Admiral Cochrane Drive. 410-573-0300
Annapolis Econo Lodge. 2451 Riva Road. 410-841-2545
Knights Inn. 69 N. Old Mill Bottom Road. 410-349-1600
Country Inns and Suites. 2600 Housley Road. 410-571-6700

Special Places Outside Annapolis To Stay

Robert Morris Inn. 312 North Morris Street. Oxford. 410-226-5111. Built before 1710. In 1738 Robert Morris, Sr. Bought the house. His son Robert Morris, Jr. helped fund the American Revolution and was a signer of the Declaration of Independence. Excellent seafood restaurant.

The Ashby 1663. Easton. 410-822-4235. Estate on Miles River. The movie "Silent Fall" was filmed here in 1993.

Gross Coate Plantation 1658. 1130 Gross' Coate Road, Easton. 800-580-0802. Once owned by Tilghman family. On Gross' and Lloyd Creeks opposite Wye Island.

White Swan Tavern. 231 High Street. Chestertown. 410-778-2300. Historic inn dating back to 1733, filled with lovely antiques.

Tidewater Inn. 101 E. Dover Street, Easton. 410-822-1300. A wonderful place for a convention or just getting away to the Eastern Shore.

Kent Manor Inn and Restaurant. Route 50 and Route 8 South. Stevensville. 1-800-820-4511 or 410-643-5757. Charming southern plantation inn built c 1820 on 226 acres of farmland on Eastern Shore.

The Inn at Perry Cabin. 308 Watkins Lane. St. Michael's. 800-722-2949. Inn owned by Laura Ashley family, located on harbor in St. Michael's.

Chapter 4

Dining

Reservations are recommended during the summer and Friday and Saturday nights. The Chesapeake is world famous for crabs, oysters, rockfish and shad, especially the roe. Unfortunately fishing for shad on the Bay has been banned. Projects are now underway to open up the many dams so that they can swim back up the rivers to spawn. Male crabs are called "jimmies', and female "sooks". Also in abundance during the summer are delicious fresh fruits and vegetables.

Where to Go for the Yachting Crowd

McGarvey's. City Dock. 410-263-5700
Pussers at the Annapolis Marriott Waterfront. 80 Compromise Street. 410-626-0004
Yacht Clubs. These are private clubs and unless you are a member or have reciprocity with your club you cannot enter.

Local Annapolis Favorites

McGarvey's. City Dock. 410-263-5700

Best Dinner

Treaty of Paris. State Circle. 410-269-0900
Maria's Italian Restaurant and Café. 12 Market Space. 410-268-2112
Restaurant Michaelangelo. 2552 Riva Road. 410-573-0970
Lewnes Steak House. 401 Fourth Street. 410-263-1617
Samson's. 136 City Dock. 410-263-3353
Fred's Restaurant. New Solomons Island Road. 410-224-2386

Best Place to Go with your Favorite Beau or Girl

Treaty of Paris. Maryland Inn. 410-263-2641
Harry Browne's. 66 State Circle. 410-263-4332

Best Place to Take your Grandmother or other Special People

Wild Orchid. 909 Bay Ridge Avenue, Eastport. 410-268-8009
Northwoods 609 Melvin Avenue. 410-268-2609

Best View

Chart House. 300 Second Street. 410-268-7166
Pusser's Landing. Marriott Hotel. 410-626-0004
Carrol's Creek Café. 410 Severn Avenue. 410-263-8102
Vespucci's. City Dock. 410-571-0100
Sam's Waterfront Café. Chesapeake Harbour. 410-263-3600
Two Seasons Café. Annapolis Landing Marina. 410-263-7247
Fergie's Waterfront Restaurant and Catering. 2840 Solomons Island Road. 410-573-1371
Mike's Restaurant and Crab house. Riva Road. 410-956-2784
Surfside 7. 48 S. River Road. 410-956-8975

Best Wine List

Treaty of Paris. Maryland Inn. 410-224-3150
Lewnes. 401 Fourth Street. 410-263-1617
Maria's. 12 Market Space. 410-268-2112

Steaks

Lewnes Steakhouse. 4th Street at Severn Avenue, Eastport. 410-263-1617. Best steaks and lobsters in town.
Ruth's Chris Steak House. 301 Severn Avenue. 410-990-0033
Governor's Grill. 177 Main Street. 410-263-6555

Seafood

McGarvey's. 8 Market Space. 410-263-5700
O'Leary's. 310 3rd Street. 410-263-0884
Cantler's. Forest Beach Road. 410-757-1311
Olde Towne. 105 Main Street. 410-268-8703
Main Street Seafood & Grill. 164 Main. 410-626-1170
McNasby's. 723 Second Street. 410-268-CRAB

Surfside 7. 48 S. River Road. 410-956-8075
Fergie's Waterfront Restaurant. Rte. 2, Edgewater. 410-573-1371
Mike's Restaurant. Riva Road on South River. 410-956-2784
Annapolis Fish Market. Market House. 410-269-0490
Calvert House. 2444 Solomons Island Road. 410-266-9210
Paul's on the South River. Riva Road. 410-956-3410

Ribs

Adams The Place for Ribs. 169 Mayo Road. Edgewater. 410-956-2995
Adams Ribs East. Eastport Shopping Center. 410-267-0064
Red Hot and Blue. 200 Old Mill Bottom Road, St. Margarets. 410-626-7427

Family Restaurants

Busch's Chesapeake Inn. Rt. 50 Exit 29. 410-757-1717

Pubs, Cafes, and Neighborhood Places

Castlebay Irish Pub. 193A Main Street. 410-626-0165
Galway Bay. 63 Maryland Avenue
Patton's Pub. Severn and Fourth Street. 410-626-2385
Café Gurus. 601 Second Street. 410-295-0601
The Galley. 303 Second Street. 410-263-5882
Davis' Pub. 400 Chester Avenue.410-268-7432
The Moon Coffee House. 137 Prince George Street. 410-280-1956

Delis

Chick & Ruth's. 165 Main Street. 410-269-6737
Regina's Continental Delicatessen. 26 Annapolis Street. 410-268-2662

Dining in an Historic Place

Middleton Tavern. 2 Market Space. 410-269-1256

Sidewalk or Terrace Dining

Middleton Tavern. 2 Market Space. 410-263-3323
Pussers. 80 Compromise Street. 410-626-0004
Riordan's. 26 Market Space. 410-263-5449
Griffins. 22 Market Space. 268-2576
McGarvey's. 8 Market Space. 410-263-5700
Market House. Opposite City Dock has a number of take out places and tables.
McNasby's. 723 Second Street. 410-268-CRAB
Henry Browne's. 66 State Circle. 410-263-4332
Potato Valley. 47 State Circle. 410-267-0902

French Cuisine

Café Normandie. 185 Main Street. 410-263-3382

Chinese

China Wok. Eastport Plaza. 410-268-1200
China House. 228 Main Street. 410-263-0002
The Canton Restaurant. 11 Ridgely Avenue. 410-280-8658
Joy Luck. 905 Bay Ridge Road. 410-263-6800

Vietnamese

Saigon Palace. 609-B Taylor Avenue. 410-268-4463
La Rose de Saigon. 960 Bay Ridge Road. 410-268-8484

Thai

Papazee's Authentic Thai Cuisine. 257 West Street. 410-263-8424

Japanese

Joss Café & Sushi Bar. 195 Main Street. 410-263-4688
Nikko. 189 A Main Street. 189 A Main Street. 410-267-6688

Italian and Mediterranean

Restaurant Michaelangelo. 2552 Riva Road. 410-573-0970
Ciao! 51 West Street. 410- 267-7912
Vespucci's. City Dock. 410-571-0100
Mangia. 81 Main Street. 410-268-1350
Aromi d'Italia. On the City Dock , next to Vespucci's. 410-263-1300
Cantina d'Italia. 2478 Solomons Island Road. 410-224-1330

Pizza

Tony's. 36 West Street. 410-268-1631

Southwestern/Mexican

Fiesta. 975 Bay Ridge Road. 410-626-1570
Eastport Clipper Cantina. 400 Sixth Street, Eastport. 410-280-6400
Armadillo's. 132 Dock Street. 410-268-6680
El Toro Bravo. 50 West Street. 410-267-5949
Arizona's. 1803 West Street. 410-263-9006

Restaurants with Music

King of France Tavern. Maryland Inn, Church Circle. 410-263-2641
Middleton Tavern. 2 Market Space. 410-263-3323
O'Brien's. 113 Main Street. 410-268-6288
Ram's Head Tavern. 33 West Street. 410-268-4545
Eastport Clipper. 400 Sixth Street, Eastport. 410-280-6400
Armidillo's Bar & Grill. 132 Dock Street. 410-268-6680
49 West Coffeehouse. 49 West Street. 410-626-9796
Franklin Street Pub at Reynolds Tavern. Church Circle. 410-626-0380
Harry Browne's. 66 State Circle. 410-263-4332
Topside Inn. Rte. 255, Galesville. 410-867-1321
Surfside 7. 48 S. River Road. Edgewater. 410-956-8075

Place to take your younger sister or brother (of legal age)

McGarvey's. 8 Market Space. 410-263-5700
O'Brien's Bar & Grill. 113 Main Street. 410-268-6288

Acme Bar & Grill. 163 Main Street. 410-280-6486

Best Place to Watch Men or Women and Good Food Too

McGarvey's. City Dock. 410-263-5700
Griffins. One Market Square. 410-268-2576
Riordans. 26 Market Space. 410-263-5449
Pussers. Marriott. 80 Compromise Street. 410-626-0004

Waterfront Bars

Pussers. 80 Compromise Street. 410-626-0004
Vespucci's. 87 Prince George Street. 410-571-0100
Chart House.300 Second Street. 410-268-7166

Crab Feasts

What better way to spend a lazy day or evening than a crab feast. Often these are hosted by churches or civic groups. Several restaurants also serve them. Look for wooden tables, lots of paper napkins. Ice and beer. Kids welcome.

Harris Crab House. Kent Narrows, Grasonville. 410-827-9500
Cantler's Riverside Inn on Mill Creek.410-757-1467
Buddy's Crabs and Ribs. 100 Main Street. 410-626-1100
David W. Wehrs Seafood. Alley Bay, Kent Island. 410-643-5778

Bagels

Einstein's Bagel. City Dock. 410-280-3500
Bruegger's Bagel Bakery. 2329 Forest Drive. 410-266-6509

Coffee

49 West Coffeehouse and Gallery. 49 West Street. 410-626-9796
City Dock Café. 18 Market Place. 410-269-0969
Starbucks Coffee. 124 Dock Street

Place to be seen for Breakfast

Chick & Ruth's. 165 Main Street. 410-269-6737
Paul's Homewood Café. 919 West Street. 410-267-7891
Main Street Seafood & Grill. 164 Main Street. 410-626-1170

Brunch

Carrol's Creek. 410 Severn Avenue, Eastport. 410-263-8102
Treaty of Paris. Maryland Inn. 410-216-6340
Schooner Liberte. 410-263-8234. Call for schedule
Annapolis Holiday Inn & Conference Center. 210 Holiday Court. 410-224-3150

Afternoon Tea

The Wild Orchid Café. 909 Bay Ridge Avenue. 410-268-8009
London Town. 839 Londontown House Road. Edgewater. 410-222-1919

Ice Cream

Storm Brothers Ice Cream Factory. 130 Dock Street
Ben & Jerry's. 139 Main Street

Better Hotel Restaurants

Treaty of Paris. Maryland Inn. 410-269-2641
Pusser's. Marriott. 80 Compromise Street. 410-626-0004
Corinthian. Loewe's Hotel. 126 West Street. 410-263-1299

Caterers, Pastry Chefs and Carry Out

Rendez-vous Catering. 2129 Forest Drive. 410-841-5688
The Palate Pleasers. 1023 Bay Ridge Avenue. 410-263-7609
Main Ingredient. 914 Bay Ridge Road. 410-626-0388
Confections of Annapolis. 53 West Street. 410-295-0459
Restaurants 2 You. 410-266-3663. Delivery service for restaurants.
Desserts Direct. 410-212-7832. Best cakes.

Ridgewell's. 5525 Dorsey Lane. Bethesda. 301- 652-1515.
Giolitti. 208 Somerville Road. 410-266-8600
Breeze Cuisine. Edgewater. 410-956-6606
Confections of Annapolis. 53 West Street. 410-295-0459
Big Cheese. Market Place. 410-263-6915
City Dock Bakery. Market house. 410-269-6361
Kaufman's Fancy Fruits and Vegetables. Market House. 410-269-0941
Mann's Sandwiches. Market House. 410-263-0644
Annapolis Global Gourmet. 914 Bay Ridge Road. 410-263-2929

Cooking Schools

The Annapolis Cooking School. 410-266-1511

Gourmet Dinner Series

The Duchess Inn. 164 Duke of Gloucester Street. 410-267-9296

Places for Special Occasions, Weddings and Garden Parties

London Town House and Gardens. 839 Londontown House Road. 410-222-1919

Quiet Waters Park. 600 Quiet Waters Park Road. 410-222-1777

Charles Carroll House. 107 Duke of Gloucester Street. 410-269-1737

William Paca House. 186 Prince George Street. 410-263-5553

Thomas Point Park. 3890 Thomas Point Road. 410-222-1969

Did You Know?

British Navy Pusser's Rum (grog) was given as a daily ration aboard British Naval vessels from 1655 to 1970. It is a blend of five West Indian rums, according to an 1810 recipe. A "Royal Navy Fog Cutter" is made of rum, brandy, gin, orange juice, lemon and Orgeat syrup over ice.

A Salty Dog is not an old sailor, but a shot of vodka with grapefruit juice served over ice in a salted glass.

A Tradewinds Breeze is a shot of vodka over ice served with equal parts of cranberry and pineapple juices.

Between the Sheets doesn't mean caught in the ropes. Rather it is one part triple sec, two parts lime juice, three parts brandy and three parts rum shaken with crushed ice and strained.

Enough for sailor's drinks. As long as it contains rum it will make for a joyful end of a day!

The earliest drinks served in the clubs were punches, especially rum, port, Spanish wine and sherry and Madeira.

The earliest known inn in Annapolis was the Kentish Inn.

Establishments that served liquor or meals, or provided lodging had to pay for an ordinary license received from the Circuit Court of Anne Arundel County. The license holder had to provide at least six beds, provender for ten or more horses. Food and liquor prices were fixed by law. An ordinary was a colonial term for inns and taverns.

Indentured servants needed permission from their masters to be served in an inn or tavern.

Out-of-town guests could not receive credit for more than 10 shillings.

Middleton Tavern, 2 Market Space, was built by Samuel Horatio Middleton in 1745 as a club. Records in 1774 show that the inn had 12 rooms, a separate kitchen and meat house. The present tavern has been run by Joseph Hardesty since 1968. James Gross has been employed here since 1948.
The Tuesday and Jockey Clubs met here. Later it was a tavern and store selling Madeira, rum, molasses, sugar, beer and even lemons.

Reynolds Tavern was opened in 1747 by William Reynolds who leased the land from St. Anne's Parish. The building has been a hattery, bank, restaurant and library. The building is owned by the National Trust for Historic Preservation, but leases it to the Historic Annapolis Foundation until 2076 for $1 per annum.

The Maryland Inn dates from 1772 and was built as a tavern and inn by Thomas Hyde.

Records show the King of France Tavern was operated by Sarah Ball in 1784.

Another watering hole founded in 1773 was the "Sign of the Indian King".

The Shiplap House, 18 Pinkney Street, during the 18th c was run as an inn by Edward Smith. In 1787 it was rented to John Humphrey as the tavern "at the Sign of the Harp and Crown".

The first coffee house was the Maryland Coffee House opened in 1767 by Cornelius Howard at 200 Main Street.

Armadillo's was once a jailhouse. The lovely brick building is over 200 years old.

O'Brien's at 113 Main Street was built in 1774, once the Rose and Crown, later Fran O'Brien's, and a bowling alley. During the 1980's unfortunately much of the building was destroyed by fire. It is now rebuilt.

Rumney's Tavern, once located at London Town, and owned by Edward and Elinor Rumney, served victuals from the 1690s until 1720, when it was taken over by Stephen West.

Earl "Fatha" Hines was one of the earliest musicians to appear at King of France Tavern. Other famous bands that have appeared in Annapolis are the Count Basie Band, Artie Shaw (he just passed away in April 1998) Band, Glenn Miller Band, and more recently the Charlie Byrd and Stef Scaggari bands. During the 1920 and 30's Carr's Beach featured Louis Armstrong, Count Basie and Duke Ellington. Big bands also played at the Naval Academy during World War II.

Sign O' the Whale

©1998

Ginger Doyl

Chapter 5

Shopping

Favorite gifts to take home are anything nautical, and seasonings such as "Old Bay" for seafood. The Annapolis artist Lee Boynton has designed some wonderful steins with Chesapeake scenes on them, and Nancy Hammond's prints are very special. Annapolis has many chain stores, but the shops listed here are unique to the town.

Men's Clothing

Johnson's "On the Avenue"- Corner Maryland Avenue and State Circle
Laurance. 232 Main Street
Fawcett Boat Supplies. 110 Compromise Street

Ladies' Clothing

Sign of the Whale - 99 Main Street
The Leader - 167 Main Street
Elanne. 27 Maryland Avenue
Fawcett Boat Supplies. 110 Compromise Street
Hazel T. 206 Main Street
Calico Mouse. 151 Main Street
Chesapeake Trading Co. 149 Main Street
The Black Market. 145 Main Street
The White House. 129 Main Street
Why Knot. 162 Main Street
Jazoo. 158 Main Street
April Cornell. 16 Market Space
Mary's Designer Boutique. 150-D Jennifer Road

Specialty Shops/Gifts

League of Maryland Craftsmen. 54 Maryland Avenue.
Plat du Jour. 220 Main Street.
Avoca Handweavers. 141 Main Street.
Sign of the Whale. 99 Main Street
Chesapeake Trading Company. 149 Main Street

The Museum Store. 77 Main Street.
Peake House. 76 Maryland Avenue.
Details. 80 Maryland Avenue.
The Pewter Chalice. 168 Main Street
Easy Street. 8 Francis Street
Annapolis Treasure Company. 161 Main Street
La Blanca Flor. 34 Market Space
La Joie de Vivre. 155-B Main Street
Pueblo Azul. Harbour Square on City Dock
Insight Concepts. 155A Main Street
Annapolis Shirt Company. 159 Street
Al Goodies Gifts. 112 Main Street
Nature Company. 134 Main Street
Annapolis Country Store. 53 Maryland Avenue
Big Iguana. 118 Dock Street
Treasures of the British Isles. 211 Main Street

Christmas Shops

Christmas Spirit. 180 Main Street

Pottery

Annapolis Pottery. 40 State Circle. 410-268-6153

Furniture

The Bartley Collection Limited. 29060 Airpark Drive, Easton. 410-820-7722.
Excellent reproduction furniture sold finished or unfinished.
Annapolis Furniture Company. 238 West Street. 410-295-7463
Hopkins Furniture Co. 123 Main Street. 410-269-0606

Antiques

There are many antique shops along Maryland Avenue, in West Annapolis, Main Street and along West Street.
Ron Snyder Antiques. 2011 West Street. 410-266-5452

Galleries

Annapolis has many fine galleries and artists, many of them painting local scenes of the Historic District or the Chesapeake Bay. Nancy Hammond is a favorite local. On a national basis Lee Boynton has done many paintings of the Bay, murals for the city's tercentenary, and in 1998 a cover for the L. L. Bean catalogue. There are also many excellent galleries on the Eastern Shore.

Nancy Hammond Editions. 64 State Circle
Annapolis Marine Art Gallery. 110 Dock Street
Dawson Gallery. 44 Maryland Avenue
Mitchell Art Gallery. St. John's College
League of Maryland Craftsmen. 54 Maryland Avenue
Gallery on the Circle. 18 State Circle
Obelyn Galleries. 194 Green Street
Ira Pinto Gallery. 6 Cornhill Street
McBride Gallery. 215 Main Street
Maryland Federation of Art. 18 State Circle
Carl Patty. 31 Maryland Avenue
Aurora Gallery. 67 Maryland Avenue
Moon Shell Gallery. 6 Fleet Street
Whitehall Gallery. 57 West Street
Main Street Gallery. 109 Main Street
Quiet Waters Park Galleries. Hillsmere Drive
La Petite Gallery. 39 Maryland Avenue
Maria's Picture Place. 45 Maryland Avenue
Jan R. Mitchell. 61 Cornhill Street
Schoenbauer Gallery. 29 Francis Street
Munro Wood Gallery. 45 West Street
West Annapolis Gallery. 108 Annapolis Street
The Galleries at Maryland Hall for the Creative Arts. 801 Chase Street

Books/Records

Briarwood Bookshop. 88 Maryland Avenue. 410-268-1440. Rare and old books. Good collection on Maryland
Naval Institute Bookstore. Naval Academy Museum. Preble Hall
Oceans II Records. 178 Main Street

Flower Shops

Flowers by James. State Circle.410-268-3341
Gateway Florist. 67 West Street. 410-263-3623
Colonial Florist. 2140 Forest Drive. 410-266-6800
Michelle's. 917 Bay Ridge. 410-263-0988
Michael. 108 Annapolis Street. 410-263-0401
Shelly's Flower Box. 260 King George Street. 410-267-0876

Stationery

Beverly's. 60 West Street. 410-263-4304
Paper Gourmet. 3 Church Circle. 410-263-8710

Hats

Hats in the Belfry. 103 Main Street

Children's Clothing/ Toys

The Giant Peach. 110 Annapolis Street. 410-268-8776

Candy Stores

Uncle Bob's Fudge Kitchen. 112 Main Street
Sweet Factory. 118 Main Street

Cigar Shops

Annapolis Cigar Company. 121 Main Street
The Smoke Shop.   56 Maryland Avenue

Markets

Graul's. Taylor Avenue at Rowe Boulevard

Picnic and Sailing Supplies

Market House. City Dock
Mangia. 81 Main Street
Einstein Bagels. 124 Dock Street
The Main Ingredient. 914 Bay Ridge Road

Seafood

Annapolis Seafoods. Forest Drive and Tyler Avenue 410-269-5380
McNashby's. 723 Second Street. Eastport. 410-280-2722

Ice Cream

Storm Brothers Ice Cream. City Dock

Liquor and Wine

Mills. 87 Main Street

Cookware/China/Linens

Plat du Jour. 220 Main Street. 410-269-1499
Palais Royal. 167 Jennifer Road. 410-224-0015
Ann Widener's Peake House. 76 Maryland Avenue. 410-280-0410

Hardware Stores

Stevens. 142 Dock Street

Malls

Annapolis Mall
Annapolis Harbour Center
Festival at Riva Road Shopping Center
Jennifer Shopping Center

Nurseries

Homestead Gardens. 743 W. Central Avenue, Davidsonville. 410-798-5000

Flags and Banners/ Kites

Kites Up & Away. 6 Fleet Street

Jewelry Shops

Tilghman Jewlers. 44 State Circle
Ron George Jewelers. 205 Main Street
La Belle Cezanne Jewelers. 117 Main Street
Zachary's Exquisite Jewelry. 122 Main Street
W.R. Chance Jewelers. 110 Main Street

Opticians

Embassy Opticians. 234 Main Street

Drugstore

Rite Aid. 609 Taylor Avenue. 410-268-5007

Camera Shop

Ritz Camera Shop. 138 Main Street. 410-263-6050

Clocks

The Ordinary Clock Shop. 12 Annapolis Street

Nameboards

The Raven Maritime Studio. 130 Severn Avenue, Eastport. 410-268-8639

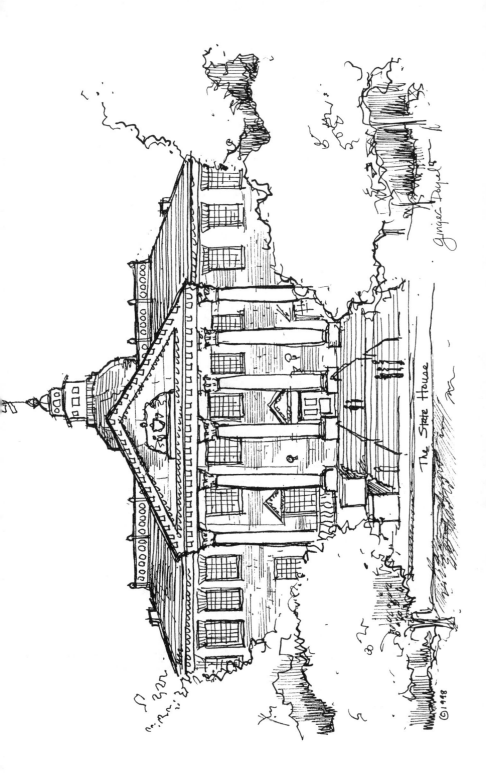

The State House

Ginger Doyle

©1998

Chapter 6

The History of Annapolis

Annapolis' unique location on the Chesapeake at the mouth of the Severn River and Chesapeake Bay played an important role in its settlement and becoming one of America's grand cities and capital. It sits on three peninsulas and has four creeks. The Bay was formed about 15,000 years ago by glaciers in the Susquehanna Valley. Most of the food came from here - fish, especially rockfish and shad, crabs, oysters from the Chesapeake and the fertile land, produced an abundance of crops.

The earliest inhabitants of the Chesapeake area were wanderers that began to settle c 1,000 BC. The creation of the bow and arrow c 500 AD and the cultivation of crops c 800 AD led to permanent villages. The Algonquin were the predominant group with the Susquehannocks just to the north.

The earliest English explorer of the Chesapeake Bay was Captain John Smith who set out in 1608 from Jamestown. George Calvert, the first Lord Baltimore, was given a grant in 1632 from King Charles I for all the land between the 40th parallel and the low water mark of the Potomac River to its source. He had hoped to found a colony in America, but only got as far as Newfoundland and found the area too cold and abandoned his project.

A second grant (probably 10-12 million acres) was given to his son Cecil Calvert, a Catholic, who left Virginia, which was an Anglican settlement. His wife, Anne Arundel, was the daughter of Lord Wardour. His brothers Leonard and George founded Maryland after sailing aboard the "Ark" and "Dove" with 140 passengers and landing at St. Clement's Island in the Potomac. He arrived in 1634 meeting with the Piscataway Indians, and bought a village, later St. Mary's City, and became the first Colonial Governor. As Lord Baltimore he could raise an army, incorporate towns, impose duties, establish courts, appoint government officials and vest titles. In return he gave the king 2 Indian arrows every Easter, and 1/5 of the precious metals mined in the colony.

Prior to that in 1631, William Claiborne established a trading post on Kent Island, just across from present day Annapolis. Because he claimed trading rights for the entire region and was also a Protestant, Governor Calvert sent out forces to claim the area for Maryland.

118 Puritan settlers were expelled from Virginia and Governor Stone of Maryland invited them to come providing they took an oath of allegiance to Lord Baltimore. They settled on Greenbury's Point (now owned by the Navy) across from Annapolis in 1648, claiming land on the south side also. The town of Annapolis was founded in 1649 at that time named Providence, then Anne Arundel Town after the wife of Lord Baltimore. The 1649 Toleration Act by Lord Baltimore provided freedom of worship for both Catholics and Anglicans. The tobacco cash crop was used to support the clergy and churches and 40 pounds of tobacco was levied per taxable inhabitant. Many slaves and indentured servants came to work for the tobacco planters. The earliest shipyard was known to have existed in the 1650's.

The first warrant survey in the city was conducted July 8, 1651 for Thomas Todd, a shipwright, for 100 acres along Spa Creek. In 1670 he received a patent for 120 acres for "Todd's Harbour" which now includes most of the downtown area.

The early settlers often had problems with the Indians. Governor Stone sent a commission of five men to sign the Treaty of 1652 beneath the tulip tree "Liberty Tree" on what is now the grounds of St. John's College with the Susquehanna Indians.

The earliest ferries began running across the South River in the 17th c. From 1653-58 Oliver Cornwell, Lord Protector and a Puritan, forced Maryland to recognize him as head of the state. Governor William Stone attacked Providence (Annapolis) at the Battle of the Severn in 1655 and was defeated. From 1654-57 the state was under the Puritan governor Captain William Fuller. The Governor's Proclamation of 1668 established 11 Ports of Entry, one being on Richard Acton's property (now Acton Place on Spa Creek) in Annapolis.

In 1684 the Assembly enacted a General Town Act specifying the town at Proctors was to be laid out on a hundred acre tract, which was divided into 100 one-acre lots. Richard Hill, a Quaker obtained 33 acres from Thomas Todd, Robert Proctor 48 acres and the Lord Proprietor 19 acres. Richard Beard was to survey the town, and stakes were laid out, but no homes were built. In 1689 the Proprietor lost control of Maryland, and King James was deposed. The throne went to William and Mary, who were Anglicans.

Until 1692 the Lords Baltimore appointed the Governors. In that year Charles Calvert, the Third Lord Baltimore, and Proprietor of Maryland, lost this right. He did retain legal right to Maryland and certain benefits and profits from the Province. Now the Royal Governor was appointed by the English Crown, and in 1692 Nehemiah Blackiston became governor and Francis Nicholson lieutenant governor. Also in that year the royal governor, Sir Lionel Copley, convened a representative assembly in St. Mary's which voted for "the Establishment of the Protestant Religion within this Province." Quakers lost their right to sit in the provincial assembly, but could maintain separate places of worship if the 40 pound tobacco tax was paid to the established church. Roman Catholics were not permitted to hold any office or celebrate mass except in private chapels.

Francis Nicholson, an Anglican, called his first meeting of the Maryland Assembly in September 1694, and the first order of business was the establishment of a new seat of government.   Two ports of entry were established, one was in Oxford on the Eastern Shore and the other at Arunedlton. He ordered the transfer of the capital from St. Mary's in 1694. He had been Lt. Governor of Virginia and with Rev. James Blair founded the College of William and Mary in 1693. He later was to return to Virginia as governor twice, rector of the College of William and Mary and chair of its governing board. He also laid out the city of Williamsburg and later became governor of South Carolina.

Annapolis was named for Princess Anne, daughter of King William, who became queen in 1702. The population was less than 200 people with about 60 houses. Governor Nicholson laid out the plan for the city which would radiate from two circles at the top of the hill, a plan used by Christopher Wren and John Evelyn in planning English cities. One circle would be religious with a church forming a compass rose and views to the harbor, the other political with government buildings (once called Public Circle), now Church and State Circles. Also in the plans were a Market-House, as well as "streets, lanes and alleys". The streets would be lined up with the points of a compass. The town still has North, South, East, West and Northeast Streets. Markets were held on Wednesdays and Saturdays. The Market House site on City Dock was later designated the official market site in 1752. This was torn down in 1858 and a new one built. City Dock was first called Nicholson's Cove, then Garrett Cove and the Dock finally in the 18th c.

As early as the 1640's Annapolis became a commercial port for tobacco and was made a Port of Entry in 1683. Charles Carroll emigrated from Ireland in 1688 and was later Lord Baltimore's agent. He was to become the wealthiest person in the colonies, followed by his son who built the Charles Carroll home and was an ardent Roman Catholic, and later a grandson. He owned between 70-80,000 acres of land in Maryland, Pennsylvania and New York, raising tobacco and later wheat. The third Carroll bequeathed his estate to his four daughters who gave it to the Redemptorists (a Catholic group founded in Italy

44

in 1732 who came to America in 1832). Charles Carroll (1737-1832) was the last of the signers of the Declaration of Independence to die.

The South River was used for shipping prior to the Revolution, and LondonTowne rivaled Annapolis in trade. It was one of three sites in Anne Arundel County designated to promote trade by the 1683 General Assembly. However, the water depth was too shallow and Annapolis took over as the port.

The first meeting of the Assembly was held in 1695 at the home of Major Edward Dorsey on Prince George Street. St. John's College was founded in 1696 as King William's School, with the Rev. Edward Butler first master, and later the fourth rector at St. Anne's Church. The first State House was completed in 1697. The State House, which was also the Court House, burned in 1704, when many official records were lost, including Gov. Nicholson's plans. The State House was rebuilt in 1772 with the first Legislature meeting here in 1779. It is the oldest in America in continuous use.

The earliest trades of Maryland were furs, tobacco, and iron ore. In 1719 the government offered 100 acres to anyone who would set up a furnace and forge iron. Tanning and shipbuilding were also important in Annapolis. Wheat after 1750 became the major export crop. A large shipyard was built by William Roberts on the northernmost part of town. Other shipbuilders were Patrick Creagh, and Galloway and Steward on the West River. The cities major trading partners were Great Britain, the other colonies and the West Indies.

The city received its present name in 1708 under the city charter granted by Queen Anne. In 1715 the right to appoint Governors of Maryland was returned to the Calvert family, the Proprietors of Maryland, and John Hart was the first of these 1715-20. The first mayor of Annapolis was Amos Garrett who died in 1727 and is buried in St. Anne's Cemetery.

Annapolis was also called the "Ancient City" and during its "Golden Age" was a very fashionable place to live and be seen. During the 1700's many families made their wealth through trade especially tobacco, and politicians came to town. Clubs were founded beginning in the mid 1700's - the Tuesday Club, Forensic Club, South River Club, the Ugly Club and Middleton Tavern which was founded as a club by Samuel Horatio Middleton. Horse racing, balls, theater, games and parties dominated the social scene. Shops prospered with a growing merchant class, large estate owners, and those attending the General Assembly. There were many watchmakers, gold and silver smiths, and later cabinet and furniture makers. Most of the luxury items were brought from England.

During the 1720's and '30's many tobacco plantation owners suffered from a depression, and began raising grains. From 1731-42 and 1746-52 Samuel Ogle was governor of the state. He introduced horse racing as a gentleman's sport, importing Arabian horses with Benjamin Tasker. The Baltimore Company was formed in the 1730's for wealthy planters to mine iron ore in the Patapsco region. The group was made up of Daniel Dulany, members of the Carroll family and Benjamin Tasker. The earliest theatre group, the Murray-Kean Company, performed in barns in 1752 producing such plays as "Othello" and "Richard III" by Shakespeare.

Thomas Bordley, one of the leaders of the Lower House of Elections brought William Parks to Annapolis in 1727 to publish The Maryland Gazette. At that time it was the only paper published in the colonies. It was taken over in 1745 by Jonas Green, a cousin of Benjamin Franklin's. Daniel Dulany, an attorney and the other leader of the house of elections wrote in 1728 "The Right of the Inhabitants to the Benefit of English Laws" stating Americans were entitled to English laws. In 1760 a stone windmill was built on the easternmost part of Annapolis and received the name "Windmill Point".

Governor Horatio Sharp (1753-69) spoke out against the Stamp Act of 1763. General Daniel Dulany wrote about its unconstitutionality in 1765 "Consideration on the Propriety of Imposing Taxes on the British Colonies, For the Purpose of Raising a Revenue", i.e. the British were taking money without the consent of the people. In that year Zachariah Hood accepted the position of Stamp Collector and a mob tore down his house. He fled to the royal troops garrisoned in New York. The winter of 1765 was a particularly cold one and the Bay froze, allowing carriages to cross to Kent Island. The Sons of Liberty was formed in 1766 by Samuel Chase and William Paca to defy Parliament by forcing the courts to act without stamps and to repeal the Stamp Act. Kunte Kinte, made famous in Alex Haley's "Roots" arrived at City Dock in 1767.

The 1767 the Townshend Act of the British government taxed glass, lead, paint, and tea. Anti importation groups formed, and the ship "Good Intent" was sent back to England. The Stamp Act of 1774 also had an impact on Annapolis. Annapolis had its own "Tea Party" when local patriots forced Anthony Stewart to destroy his vessel, the Peggy Stewart, with a cargo of 2,000 pounds of English tea and other goods by running her aground in Spa Creek and setting fire to her. Some families did remain loyal to the Crown, such as the Dulanys, Ridouts and Ogles, with several leaving for England during the Revolution.

In 1775 900 "displaced" persons (by the British) from Nova Scotia came by ship to Annapolis, settling here and in Baltimore, bringing their own style of architecture. A 1776 map published in England showed that Annapolis had about 150 homes.

During the Revolutionary War many Annapolitans served under General Washington, and many boats sailed from the harbor. Three Annapolitans signed the Declaration of Independence in 1776 - William Paca, Samuel Chase and Charles Carroll. Charles Carroll chaired the committee to write the State Constitution, which included the election of governors for one year. The first governor was Thomas Johnson, who had recommended George Washington as Commander-in-Chief of the Continental Army, and who later became a Justice of the Supreme Court and helped plan the city of Washington. In July 1776 Maryland issued its own declaration of independence.

Lafayette and Comte de Rochambeau and the French fleet several times passed through Annapolis beginning in 1781, making it a base. The French troops encamped on Dorsey Creek, now College Creek, and Lafayette on Spa Creek in Eastport. The two Frenchmen were to return to Annapolis after Cornwallis' surrender. In 1782 William Paca became Governor of Maryland.

1783 was a very important year for Annapolis. The importation of slaves was forbidden by Maryland Law. Capt. Joshua Barney, who had distinguished himself in many Naval battles, and a native of Baltimore, arrived from Paris with a provisional Treaty of Paris. Annapolis was offered to Congress as a permanent home in October by Mayor Jeremiah Townley Chase, which turned out to be only temporary until 1784. Willam Paca began his second term as Governor. On December 23, 1783 the Commander-in-chief of the Continental Army, General George Washington resigned his commission as Commander at the State House. For the first time a flag with thirteen stars was designed by the noted Annapolis cabinet maker John Shaw. Unlike the later flag with the stars in a circle this had 4,5,4 in rows. (A copy hangs in the State House). The Treaty of Paris was ratified in the same room on January 14, 1784 officially ending the Revolutionary War. In 1787 the Annapolis Convention was convened for meetings on the Articles of Confederation.

After the Revolutionary War and until the opening of the Naval Academy, Annapolis lay dormant. Baltimore took over as Maryland's port in the 1790's, and there was even word that the capital might be moved there also.

Annapolis was cut-off in 1813 when a squadron of British Royal Naval vessels began the blockade of the Chesapeake and Delaware Bays during the War of 1812. This war, declared by President James Madison came all too quickly after the Revolution to a country unprepared and financially getting on its feet. The war grew out of Britain and France's assaults against each other and the fact each wanted to subvert America's trade. In order to do this sailors were impressed after random checks could be made of neutral ships. In 1808 the H.M.S. Leopard attacked the U.S.S. Chesapeake. The "Chesapeake's" captain refused the random check, and she was shot at broadside by a British vessel and three men were killed. The Chesapeake was unable to defend herself, so the captain ended up striking her colors and four men were impressed.

Fort Severn (later the sight of the U.S. Naval Academy) was built on Windmill Point on a primitive fortified site from the Revolution. In addition Americans thought Canada might be an easy catch. Battles were fought on land and sea, with the British blockading the Chesapeake. In 1813 the towns of Frenchtown and Havre de Grace were burned by British Admiral George Cockburn. Baltimore, Annapolis and Washington were also targeted. Washington and the White House were burned, and "The Star Spangled Banner" was written by Francis Scott Key, a graduate of St. John's College, Annapolis, on the night of September 14th, as he watched the bombardment over Baltimore.

Following the War, tobacco growing declined, but shipbuilding became an important industry. The first steamboats began arriving after 1813. The 1830 census showed Annapolis had a population of 2,623 people. In 1840 the Annapolis and Elkridge Railroad opened allowing transportation between Washington and Annapolis. The famous Liberty Tree at St. John's College, under which the Sons of Liberty had met before and during the Revolutionary War, had its trunk hollowed when some boys placed gunpowder in it and caught fire (1840). Annapolis was linked to the main line of the Baltimore and Ohio Railroads on Christmas Day 1840. The opening of the Naval School in 1845, later the U.S. Naval Academy, brought an awakening to the city. St. Anne's Church was reconstructed in 1859 after a fire destroyed it the previous year. The building, the present one, cost $21,500 and the steeple $8,000. In that year the Annapolis Gas-Light Company was founded.

By 1860 the population of Annapolis had grown to 4,658, free blacks 1,056 and 475 slaves. During the Civil War, like the Revolution, people had divided loyalties, some to the Confederacy, others to the Union. Slavery had played an important role in growing tobacco, but with its decline slaves were freed, many living in Annapolis or settling on the Eastern Shore as watermen. Maryland was a slave-holding state under its Constitution, but remained loyal to the Union under Gov. Thomas Hicks. In 1861 the Naval Academy students were moved to Newport, RI and St. John's College became the College Green Hospital in 1863, Hospital #2, and the Naval Academy Hospital #1. During the War northern troops were located at Horn Point (in Eastport) and later camped at the Naval Academy. Annapolis was occupied by Massachusetts troops under General Benjamin F. Butler. General Winfield Scott appointed Gen. Butler

Commander of the City of Annapolis on April 27, 1861 and then elevated him to Command of the Department of Annapolis, which included about 20 miles radiating in all directions from the city.

With the Emancipation Proclamation in 1864 only slaves in states "in rebellion against the United States" were freed. Maryland had to write a new Constitution to free them. The schools were segregated until the 1950's, the library until the '40's.

Oystering began in earnest during the Civil War, and was to reach its peak in the 1870's with more than 11 million bushels accounted for. During this time the oystermen of Maryland and Virginia staked out claims on the Bay, which was not settled till 1877 when boundaries were set.

The first bridge across Spa Creek was built in 1868, when Eastport was first laid out. It extended from the Bay to Sixth Street, and was not annexed to Annapolis until 1951. Much of the area was farmland, the people oystermen or ship builders. During the winter of 1876-77 the harbor froze over and many boats were frozen in. A fire burned the block between Main and Cornhill Streets on Market Space in 1883 costing $90,000. By 1888 the town had four public schools, separated by race and sex; 3 parochial schools and five private.

1901 was a winter not to be forgotten when the Bay froze from December 22 to March 20. In 1902 and 1904 there were other major fires. The next bridge to Eastport was built in 1907. From 1908-35 a trolley of the Washington, Baltimore and Annapolis electric line ran on downtown streets. (trolley tracks are still noticeable under the pavement) McDowell Hall at St. John's burned in 1909. In 1910 the Emergency Hospital opened, heated with hot water and electricity, and the first female doctor, Francis E. Weitzman, arrived in 1912 from Philadelphia. The worst storm in Annapolis' history struck on August 14, 1915 destroying bridges, flooding downtown and leaving the city paralyzed for several days.

Annapolis was declared a "dry zone" in 1918 by the Secretary of the Navy. No liquor was to be sold within a five mile radius of any naval facility. Saloons were fined up to $1000 or jail for one year. For a town that had relied on its many taverns this was devastating news.

The first ferry boat to carry autos to the Eastern Shore was launched in 1919, the Governor Emerson C. Harrison. The original wooden bridge over the Severn River was not replaced until 1924.

The 1930 census showed 12,531 people. During the 1930's and '40's one of the more popular places in town was the Capitol Restaurant and Hotel at 200 Main. One of the most ferocious storms to come up the Chesapeake occurred in 1933, when a tropical storm brought a strong northwesterly wind and the very highest tides ever recorded.

The present Spa Creek Bridge was installed in 1947 at a cost of $667,000. The last passenger train departed in 1950. Ferry service across the Bay was discontinued in 1952 with the opening of the first span of the Bay Bridge (the William Preston Lane Bridge, named for the governor 1947-51). The single span bridge begun in 1949, cost $112 million and is 4.2 miles long. Beginning in 1997 painting the bridge will cost $79 million.

The Historic Annapolis Foundation was founded in 1952 when several concerned citizens realized the State had appropriated $950,000 to purchase 14 buildings on State Circle, School and Main Streets, and was going to raze them to make way for a 100,000 square foot office building. The Carroll Barrister House was also saved when it was supposed to be torn down in 1954 for the new telephone company building. Mrs. J.M.P. Wright is rightfully called "The Godmother of Historic Annapolis" for her efforts to spearhead this group. The Shiplap House, also "rescued", became the headquarters for the Foundation. Hurricane Hazel ripped through Annapolis in 1954 putting City Dock and some of downtown once again under water.

Until the 1960's much of the Annapolis area and its surrounding environs was lovely farmland. Bowie Farm still harvested tobacco, now Annapolis Cove. In 1962 the John Hanson Highway (Route 50) was completed to Washington. The center part of the old city was designated a "Registered National Historic Landmark" in 1965 because of the importance of the pre Revolutionary buildings.

The government has built many new office buildings, and the town has expanded way beyond its original boundaries. Townhouses, palatial homes on the rivers, shopping malls and highways leave little room for growth. Some of the major issues pending legislation focus on the preservation of the Chesapeake Bay. The Chesapeake Bay Foundation was founded in 1987 when the governors of Maryland, Virginia and Pennsylvania agreed to "Save the Bay". Likewise zoning and preserving this small peninsula are of great concern to the citizens of Annapolis, and though tourism has become a major industry, maintaining the beauty and history of the town is necessary.

Did You Know

Anne Arundel County is named for Lady Anne Arundel, wife of Cecilius Calvert, second Lord Baltimore. The area was first called Providence. It was laid out in hundreds, and when the Church of England was established here, in parishes. St. Mary's City was the first capital, and Larkin Hill a temporary capital in 1683. Larkin Hill, now located on Rte. 2 was the site of a meeting in 1682 between Charles, Lord Baltimore and William Penn to discuss the boundaries of Pennsylvania and Maryland. Annapolis became the capital of Maryland in 1696 under Governor Nicholson.

Liberty Trees received their name from those men that defied the British Stamp Act during the Revolution, and gathered under a designated tree for meetings. In Annapolis Samuel Chase chose the one now known as "The Liberty Tree", a tulip poplar, on St. John's campus. The Annapolis Liberty Tree is used on the plaques of the Historic Annapolis Foundation to designate historic buildings and homes.

The State Flag of Maryland is the Calvert family colors, yellow, and black, and the Crossland red and white. Crossland was the family name of the first Lord Baltimore's mother. The flag was officially adopted as the state flag in 1904. The State Seal consists of a shield with the Calvert and Crossland arms quartered. Above is an earl's coronet and helmet. The shield has on one side a farmer and on the other a fisherman. The Calvert motto on the scroll is "Fatti maschli parole femine". The Latin on the border is translated as " with favor wilt thou compass us as a shield", the last verse of Psalm 5. The date 1632 is when Lord Baltimore was granted a charter for the colony.

Maryland was named for Queen Henrietta Maria, wife of Charles I of England who granted the charter to found the colony to the first Lord Baltimore, George Calvert, land of 6.7 million acres. Although it is said St. Mary's City and County were named for the Virgin Mary.

Transportation across the Bay and on the rivers once was by any means of boat possible. The earliest ferries crossed the South River in the 1600's to swap furs for supplies. Tobacco was an important crop by 1640 turning Annapolis into a commercial port. In the 1760's a schooner was run from Annapolis by Samuel Middleton and ferry service from Kent Island by James Hutchings. Other services went to Rock Hall and other points on the Eastern Shore. During the 1830's steamboats crossed the Bay. Annapolis to Claiborne. Ferry service under Governor Emerson C. Harrington started in June 1919. The 201 foot sidewheeler was named for the governor. She was followed by the double-ender Governor Albert C. Ritchie, which also accommodated cars. In 1930 the terminus was moved to Matapeake. During the ealy 1900's the sidewheeler "Emma Giles" docked in Annapolis at the Prince George Street Wharf and was used for week-end excursions to Baltimore and the Eastern Shore.

Increased interest in the beaches brought more traffic. The first span of the Bay Bridge was begun in 1948. Today two parallel bridges expand the Bay just north of Annapolis. Beginning in 1997 the Bridges will be painted, a job costing $76 million, more than the original cost of the bridges!

On February 10, 1948 The Maryland State Roads Commission announced plans to build a dual highway between Washington and Annapolis to link up with the new Bay Bridge via a crossing across the Severn River. Today Route 50 is three or more lanes wide.

Route 2 – Crain Highway- which went from Baltimore to Annapolis became known as "Bootleg Boulevard" during Prohibition as "hooch" was smuggled along here, The area between the Severn River and Sandy Point was notorious for "moonshine" making during Prohibition. Even Gov. Ritchie was against the 18th Amendment that brought about 14 years of Prohibition.

Crain Highway was named for Robert Crain who helped bring the Democratic Convention to Baltimore in 1912 when Woodrow Wilson was nominated.

Route 2, Solomon's Island Road was originally an Indian trail, following the ridge dividing streams of the Patuxent River and the Rhode and West Rivers. This was the first postal route between Annapolis and St. Mary's City.

Rev. J. Pinkney Hammond during the Civil War wrote the song "Stand By the Flag Boys".

The Chesapeake is the largest bay in the country. Rockfish is the official state fish.

The Chesapeake Bay Retriever has been the official dog of Maryland since 1964. (The author's grandfather raised these dogs on Harmony Hills Farm, now a horse breeding farm in Havre de Grace).

Alex Haley, author of "Roots" found that his ancestor, Kunta Kinte from Gambia, was listed on the roster of the British ship "Lord Ligonier" in 1767, and was sold into slavery on City Dock.

The painter, Charles William Peale (1741-1827), was born in St. Anne's County, and later was apprenticed to a saddler in Annapolis. He painted signs for which he received recognition. In 1767 he was sent to London to study under Benjamin West by his patron William Paca. He painted the portraits of George Washington and William Pitt that hang in the State House. Other notable paintings were of William Buckland, William Paca, the Edward Lloyd Family, plus many others. Mr. Peale moved to Philadelphia in 1776, and became of America's most noted painters.

James Peale, brother of Charles, also was a noted painter and lived in Annapolis, before joining his brother in Philadelphia. He painted many miniatures until his eyesight failed him in 1818.

The earliest painter in Annapolis was Justus Englehardt Kuhn, a German immigrant whose first records appear about 1708. He painted many of the area's well-to-do families such as the Carrolls.

Gustavus Hesselius, born in Sweden, moved to Prince Georges County sometime before 1826. He painted Thomas Bordley, Mrs. Charles Carroll and the Darnall family. He too moved to Philadelphia. His son, John, was also to paint in Maryland, Delaware and Virginia. In 1763 he married Mary Young Woodward, the widow of Henry Woodward of Primrose Hill, an estate near Annapolis. He painted such people as the Calverts, Samuel Chew and Mrs. Richard Galloway.

The other prominent Annapolis painter was John Wollaston who arrived here about 1752 from London. He too painted many famous Maryland families.

Annapolis, like Newport, Boston, Philadelphia, Baltimore and New York had its share of fine furniture makers. John Shaw was born in Scotland and came to Annapolis in 1763. His beautiful Chippendale-Federal style furniture graced all the prominent Maryland homes and the State House. His shop on Church Street, now Main, was shared with Archibald Chisholm, another Scotman. Shaw not only produced fine furniture, but was an esteemed member of the community, serving in the Revolutionary War, on the vestry of St. Anne's Church and as a city commissioner.

Among the noted craftsmen were the silversmith William Faris, Sr. and his sons. He was born in London and came to Philadelphia in 1729, moving to Annapolis in 1757. His shop on West Street produced elegant silver pieces, many of which are now displayed at Winterthur, The Metropolitan Museum of Art, and the Baltimore Museum of Art.

During the mid 1700s seventeen clubs thrived in Annapolis. The Tuesday Club was founded in 1745 by Dr. Alexander Hamilton who had come from Scotland in 1739. This was a place for men to drink ale, smoke tobacco and amuse each other, often with music. Dr. Hamilton married Margaret Dulany, daughter of Daniel Dulany. The Homony Club, founded in 1770, met at the Coffee House. The Forensic Club on Duke of Gloucester Street.

In 1896 Richard H. Green, Jr. bookkeeper of the Farmer's Bank embezzled $20,000 and ran away to his mistress of 10 years, Martha Straitiff. He had only been married for one week to Helen Claire Emory. When Ms. Straitiff found out about his marriage she turned him in, after the new Mrs. Green told authorities where she thought he was hiding!

Capt. William Mitchell (an early Marylander) was fined 5,000 pounds of tobacco for adultery and the woman 39 lashes!

The Brice House is thought to have several ghosts. Thomas Jennings Brice, son of James Brice, the builder of the house, was said to have died after being struck with a fire poker in the library. One of his slaves disappeared, but sometimes reappears. When electricity was installed in the house, a secret staircase was found going from the library to a room downstairs. In the stairwell was the skeleton of a woman. Supposedly she had gone insane, and since insanity was not acceptable she had been boarded away.

David Huxler of Kent Island was fined 25 pounds for an incestuous marriage in 1744!

The "Annapolis Riot" occurred on July 5, 1847 when the ferry boat "The Jewess" arrived overloaded from Baltimore on its way to St. Michael's. The captain feared going any further. Since the 4th had fallen on Sunday festivities for the celebration were postponed a day. When the crowd arrived the Annapolitans were furious that this group was going to upset their plans, and the Baltimorans were upset they had not been taken to St. Michael's. Several stories tell of bricks being flung at the boat, and guns were fired by a militia group on board, injuring several. A cannon used for the 4th was brought down from St. John's college, but supposedly it was not fired. No one was ever charged for misconduct!

Benedict Calvert (1724-88), the illegitimate son of Charles Calvert, fifth Lord Baltimore, immigrated to Maryland in 1742, living on Francis Street. He married his cousin Elizabeth Calvert, daughter of Gov. Charles Calvert and lived at Calvert House on State Circle. He later moved to Mount Airy in Prince George's County, and was a planter with over 20,000 acres.

Maryland was one of the most religiously liberal colonies and even with the Provincial Assembly in 1649 freedom of worship was permitted. The "Act of Toleration" fined, banished or whipped those who were not tolerant.

Henry Winter Davis was very influential in Congress before and during the Civil War, elected on the Know-Nothing ticket from Maryland. He cast the deciding vote in 1860 to permit the Republicans to organize the House of Representatives, and was later censured by the Maryland Legislature for this act.

Gov. Theodore McKeldin nominated Gen. Dwight D. Eisenhower for President at the 1952 Republican Convention.

Gov. Albert Ritchie was once considered as a presidential contender.

Until the Jew Bill of 1826 proposed by Thomas Kennedy, the Constitution of Maryland required officeholders to swear a Christian oath, thus barring Jews and people of other denominations from holding public offices.

The first movies came to Annapolis about 1890 and played at the Lyric Theatre on Market Space.

Watermen is probably an English term for the hard working fishermen of the Chesapeake.

Oystermen are tongers or dredgers "drudgers"

Tongs have been around since c 1700. They look like a double rake with a basket.

Patent tongs were invented by Charles L. Marsh, a blacksmith on the Patuxent River, in 1887. These operated remotely with a winch, and could get into deeper places with less effort.

A hydraulic tong was patented in 1958 by William Barrett and T. Rayner Wilson.

The skipjack is an exclusive Chesapeake design from the old Indian dug-out sailing canoes. They were first used in the 1890's to dredge oysters. Dredging with gasoline powered push boats is permitted Monday and Tuesdays and under sail the other days. A dredge is dragged over the oyster beds (bars) to loosen them with a dredge bag attached to catch them.

Crabbing became a major industry on the Bay in the 1870's, reaching its peak in 1920 with 50 million pounds. The best season for crabs is in the spring.

The Chesapeake has two types of clams- hard and soft-shelled or manninose.

The first horse races held in Maryland were in Annapolis in 1721. The Earl of Godolphin imported a bay stallion in 1730 from which many of Maryland's famous race horses were to trace their lineage. In 1743 the Maryland Jockey Club was formed in Annapolis, and in 1747 Governor Samuel Ogle introduced the breeding of thoroughbred horses. Race meets were held in the spring and fall. In 1752 Selime, daughter of the Godolphin horse, owned by Benjamin Tasker of Belair, beat several Virginia horses. In 1753 Governor Horatio Sharpe owner of Othello and Selima owned by Mr. Tasker produced Selim. This great horse went on to win many races owned by Samuel Galloway of Tulip Hill on the West River. George Washington was a frequent observer of these races.

In 1870 Pimlicio was opened with help from Governor Oden Bowie. The "Preakness" was to be named for one of the finest races in that year and won by Preakness. The Preakness was first run in 1873, and won by Survivor. The Kentucky Derby was founded two years later.

Sandy Point Park is on land once owned by Sylvester Labrot. Known as "Holly Beach Farm" it encompassed 2500 hundred acres on which horses were bred. The area (657 acres) around Sandy Point was purchased from William Labrot by the state of Maryland for a park in 1949 for $160,000. Mr. William Labrot made his fortune manufacturing creosol. He also owned Lee Airport and the property where Westinghouse presently is located.

The closest thing Annapolis now has to horse racing is Roedown held annually in April.

On May 6, 1898 the US gunboat "Annapolis", on blockade duty of Havana, Cuba. Captured the French mail steamer "Lafayette" as it attempted to run the blockade into Cuba. The prize crew from another US Navy ship took the steamer to Key West, Florida.

Jousting first took place in St. Mary's when the first settlers arrived in Maryland. Tournaments now take place at Christ Church, Charles County and beginning in 1998 at St. Margaret's Episcopal Church, Westminster Parish. The St. Margaret's tournement was founded by Folger McKinsey Ridout, a descendant of the Ridout family of Annapolis.

Famous Citizens of Annapolis

Charles Carroll "The Settler" was a lawyer in England and came to Maryland as Attorney General in 1688. However he lost his position almost immediately since he was a Roman Catholic and King William, a Protestant had become king. He settled in Annapolis in 1701 after living on the Eastern Shore. He received an appointment as a judge under Charles Calvert, third Lord Baltimore. He purchased property along Spa Creek and by 1716 owned ¼ of Annapolis. When he died in 1720 he owned 47,000 acres of land, the largest landowner in Maryland.

Dr. Charles Carroll was raised as a Roman Catholic, eventually becoming a Protestant. He moved to Annapolis from England c 1715. He began importing English goods and acquiring land. In 1718 he bought 2400 acres from Charles Carroll "The Settler", a cousin and eventually acquired 31,259 acres. He lived at Church (now Main) and Conduit Streets.

Charles Carroll was born in 1702 and educated in England. He built the first brick house on Spa Creek and later Doughoreagan Manor in Howard County on 10,000 acres.

Charles Carroll of Carrollton was born in 1737 and was sent to France to be educated with his second cousin, John Carroll, the first Roman Catholic Bishop of the United States. He later studied law in England and returned to Annapolis in 1765. He married Molly Darnall. They were to add onto and change the family house on Duke of Gloucester Street to a more Georgian home and built a seawall along Spa Creek. Mr. Carroll was elected to the first Maryland Senate, while also having a seat in the Continental Congress, commuting to Philadelphia 1777-1779. He was later to serve as a US Senator in the first Congress. He lived to 1832, aged 95, the last of the Signers of the Declaration of Independence.

Charles Caroll of Carrollton's son married Harriet Chew, daughter of the Chief Justice of Pennsylvania. The wedding present from his father was land in Baltimore where he built Homewood in 1801.

Daniel Dulany (1685-1753) came to Port Tobacco as an indentured servant in 1703. Under George Plater he began an apprenticeship as a lawyer. He began acquiring land and by 1720 owned 27,200 acres. In 1720 he moved to Annapolis, and here worked on the issue of rights for Maryland citizens and in 1728 wrote "The Rights of the Inhabitants of Maryland". He founded Frederick

Town and along with Benjamin Tasker and Charles Carroll of Carrollton owned the Baltimore Iron works. His home in Annapolis was off Church Circle, now the site of the County Court House.

Samuel Chase built the Chase-Lloyd House, but ran out of money, whereupon it was bought by Edward Lloyd IV. Mr. Chase was a Signer of the Declaration of Independence, served in the Continental Congress, the Maryland House of Delegates 1777, and on the Supreme Court 1796.

William Paca was born in 1740 and married Mary Chew. She and her sister Margaret who married John Beale Bordley, inherited Wye Island on the Eastern Shore, 2,795 acres from their brother Philemon Lloyd Chew. Mr. Paca built the elegant Palladian house on Wye Island, Wye Hall which burned in 1879. Mrs. Paca died in 1774 and Mr. Paca moved to Philadelphia. William Paca was elected to the Maryland Senate in 1776 and 1778. Mr. Paca was remarried to Ann Harrison of Philadelphia in 1777 and she died in 1780. Their beautiful Annapolis home on King George Street was sold to attorney Thomas Jenings in 1780. In 1782 he was elected Governor of Maryland. In 1783 Mr. Paca welcomed George Washington to Annapolis for his resignation from the Continental Army and hosted a dinner at Mann's Tavern followed by a ball at the State House. At that time the Governor's house was on Hanover Street, now near the Naval Academy Chapel. In 1786 he was elected to the lower house of the Maryland Assembly and in 1789 Judge of the US district Court for the District of Maryland.

John Shaw arrived in Annapolis in 1763 from Glasgow and worked for John Brice. He started business as a cabinet maker and in 1770 formed a partnership with Archibold Chisholm. Much of their work was for Edward Lloyd and later furnishings for the State House. John Shaw completed work on the Capital dome with the acorn on the pinnacle as a symbol of wisdom. He was named State Armorer in 1777. Mr. Shaw lived in the lovely Shaw House on State Circle.

Jonas Green in the 1730s moved from Boston to Philadelphia to work for Benjamin Franklin. In 1738 Gov. Samuel Ogle met with Benjamin Franklin in Philadelphia and mentioned the need for a printer and newspaper in Annapolis, which Jonas Green accepted. He founded the Maryland Gazette. Although he did not build the Jonas Green House it is an outstanding example of colonial architecture and where the paper was printed. Following his death his wife Anne Catherine became editor. She had fourteen children!

58

Ginger Doyle

Hammond Harwood House

©1998

Chapter 7

Buildings and Places

Annapolis is considered one of America's architectural gems, and has some of the finest brick and colonial homes. It was very fortunate that many of the grandest homes were designed by William Buckland, an architect who had come from England in 1755 as an indentured servant. He was first employed by George Mason at Gunston Hall, and then came to Annapolis in 1772. He designed the Hammond-Harwood House c 1774, the James Brice House 1777, and Strawberry Hill, all in the Palladian style of architecture. He was thought to have designed Tulip Hill c 1756 on the West River, Governor Eden's mansion, the Chase-Lloyd House 1771-73, Governor Sharp's White Hall 1764-65, and the Senate Chamber 1772.

Annapolis owes much to Mrs. A. St. Claire Wright who founded the Historic Annapolis Foundation and was able to preserve so much of this city's beautiful architecture. The HAF also has an Archeology Field Program which has worked on over 30 projects since the 1950's. The Historic District Ordinance was passed in 1969 when a group wanted to tear down the historic Market House on City Dock. Marion and Mame Warren also have preserved this in their research, pictures and books on Annapolis.

Unfortunately two devastating fires hit Annapolis, one on December 9,1997 when several buildings on Main Street and State Circle burned, and the other March 24, 1998. The latter fire on Duke of Gloucester gutted an historic home, which was the city's first synagogue. Fires are obviously a main concern of historic districts, and even with modern equipment, older buildings whether they be brick or wood are easy targets.

Historical Markers

Many of the historic homes and buildings have plaques on them that signify the period they were built. The marker's design is the Liberty Tree found at St. John's College.

Dark Green	1684-1700	17th c Vernacular
Brick Red	1700-1784	18th c Vernacular
Bronze	1735-1790	Georgian
Blue	1784-1840	Federal

Light Green	1820-1860	Greek Revival
Purple	1837-1901	Victorian
Gray	1837-1930	19th/ 20th C Vernacular
Yellow	1901-	20th c Distinctive

The State Capital

The State House is on the highest elevation in the city. The first State House was called Stadt House in deference to Dutch King William, husband of Queen Anne, and was built 1696-98. This burned in 1704 and a new one of brick was built in 1707. The old State House was torn down in 1771. The present Maryland State Capital was built in 1772 for 7200 pounds sterling, and designed by Joseph Horatio Anderson. The Legislature first met in 1779. It is the oldest state capital in continuous use. The dome, designed by Joseph Clark, was completed in 1788, and is the largest wooden dome in the country and is built without the use of nails. A new colonial revival wing was added between 1902-05.

The building has witnessed many important events in the history of the United States and Maryland. Here General George Washington tendered his resignation in the Continental Army on December 23, 1783. The Treaty of Paris, signaling the end of the Revolution, was signed January 14, 1784. It was the seat of the Continental Congress November 27, 1783 to August 9, 1784, the year Thomas Jefferson was appointed Minister Plenipotentiary. In 1786 the Annapolis Convention issued a call to the states for a Constitutional Convention, which was to lead to the eventual ratification of the Constitution in 1787 in Philadelphia and the election of George Washington as the nation's first President in 1789. This convention was held at Mann's Tavern. Maryland was the seventh state to ratify the Constitution on April 28, 1788.

The General Assembly meets January to April. The State Legislature is bicameral with 141 members in the House of Delegates and 47 members of the Senate. The offices of the Governor and Lt. Governor are on the second floor, with the House of Delegates and Senate chambers on the first. The governor and legislators are elected for four year terms.

The State House has many treasures among them items used aboard the USS Maryland such as the silver punch bowl and cups designed by Samuel Kirk and Sons, Inc. of Baltimore. The Peale family painted many prominent Annapolitans and Charles Wilson Peale's "Washington (and Gen. Lafayette and Col. Tench Tilghman) at the Battle of Yorktown", plus portraits of five Maryland Governors hang here. The painting of Thomas Johnson

61

commemorates the man who proposed George Washington to be Commander-in-Chief of the Continental Army and was elected governor 1777-79 under the Constitution of 1776. George Washington wrote that Annapolis was "the genteelist city in North America". The Flag Room is said to have the oldest U.S. flag made in accordance of an Act of Congress. The flag was carried at the Battle of Cowpens by the Third Maryland Regiment under John Eager Howard. The thirteen star flag, each with eight points was designed by John Shaw, the noted cabinetmaker who also designed the furniture used in the Old Senate chamber. Tours of the State House are available at 11AM and 3PM.

On the grounds of the State House are cannons of the Ark and Dove, the ships that brought the first settlers to St. Mary's in 1634. The statue of John Baron DeKalb (1721-80) commemorates the Revolutionary War hero. He was born in Bayreuth, Germany and joined the French army as a Knight of the Royal Order of Military Merit and Brigadier. While in Paris, he met Benjamin Franklin who encouraged him to join the American Revolution. DeKalb persuaded Marquis Lafayette to also come fight the American cause. Major General DeKalb of the U.S. Army commanded the Second Maryland Brigade in the Battle of Camden, South Carolina in 1780. He died with 11 wounds. The U.S. Congress voted to erect the memorial to him, sculpted by Ephraim Keyser.

Another statue on the State House grounds is of Roger B. Taney, Attorney General of the U.S. 1831 and Chief Justice of the United States Supreme Court 1836-64. He studied and practiced law in Annapolis, and married Ann Key, sister of Francis Scott Key. The statue in the courtyard on the Rowe Boulevard side of the State House is of Thurgood Marshall - U.S. Supreme Court Justice, appointed by Lyndon B. Johnson 1967-1991.

Other Public Buildings

The Old Treasury and Council Chamber. State Circle. Built by Patrick Creagh 1735. Oldest public building still standing in Maryland

The Maryland State Law Library. 361 Rowe Blvd. Established in 1862 it has over 300 volumes of books, the Maryland Women's Hall of Fame, law books, and a complete set of John James Audubon's "Birds of America", also called the"Elephant Books".

Anne Arundel County Courthouse. Church Circle. First built 1824, rebuilt 1892, 1925. New addition was completed 1997.

Post Office. Church Circle. Built 1901

City Hall. Duke of Gloucester Street. During the 1760's these were Assembly Rooms. It was burned during the Civil War, but the walls were used for present building.

Anne Arundel Medical Center. Cathedral Street. Founded 1902 as Annapolis Emergency Hospital. Originally in a farmhouse it had nine beds and an annual budget of $5,760. Private rooms were $12 a week and ward rooms $5!!! The present building was opened in 1930. In 1984 104 acres were purchased on Jennifer Road to expand the hospital's facilities. This was completed in 1989.

Most Beautiful Georgian and Palladian Style Houses in Annapolis

William Paca House and Gardens. Prince George Street. 410-263-5553. Home of Signer of the Declaration of Independence, three term Maryland delegate to the Continental Congress and Governor of Maryland. He also gave arms and ammunition to the American troops and outfitted a ship against the British. The house was built 1763-65 and has magnificent gardens. The house has 37 rooms and was the first Palladian style house built in Annapolis. The Carvel Hall Hotel was built in the gardens 1903-64 and demolished 1964-65. The Historic Annapolis Foundation raised $125,000 to save the house, and the State gave $330,000 for the gardens in 1965. It was not to open until ten years later.

Chase-Lloyd House. 22 Maryland Avenue. Built for Samuel Chase, signer of the Declaration of Independence and Supreme Court Justice. Completed by Edward Lloyd IV, a planter, in 1763 who at the time lived at Wye Plantation. His wife Elizabeth Tayloe Lloyd was the daughter of Col. John Tayloe who owned Mt. Airy. Their daughter married Francis Scott Key here in 1802, and in 1809 their son Edward Lloyd V became Governor of Maryland. Edward Lloyd V sold the house to his brother-in-law, Henry Hall Harwood in 1826. It has a cantilevered staircase, beautiful windows (including the largest Palladian window in the U.S.) and gardens. Willed by Hester Ann Chase Ridout to a self-perpetuating Board of Trustees, whose members had to be Episcopalians and has served as a home for elderly ladies since 1886.

235 King George Street. Part of Chase-Lloyd House. Was probably used as its summer kitchen.

James Brice House. 42 East Street. Built 1767-73 for James Brice, a colonel in the Revolution, Mayor of Annapolis and Acting Governor of Maryland in 1792. He married Juliana Jennings whose father, Thomas Jennings bought the Paca House in 1781, and who was Attorney General of the Province of Maryland. Their daughter Ann married Vachel Denton, a mayor of Annapolis. His daughter Rachel married Philip Hammond, whose son was Mathias Hammond, builder of the Hammond-Harwood House. The property was acquired in 1873 by Thomas Martin, Mayor of Annapolis. His family sold the house in 1911 for the Carvel Hotel. It is now owned by the International Masonry Institute. This gracious Georgian home has a 90 foot high chimney, the walls are three feet thick, the endwalls six feet thick.

Ridout Row - built 1774 and known as the Ridout Tenements by John Ridout. The middle house (112 Duke of Gloucester) was sold after his death to his mother-in-law Anne Tasker Ogle, who later leased it to her daughter Ann and son-in-law John Gibson, Jr. The house was auctioned in 1810, and sold to John Brewer in 1811 for $625. The house was sold upon his death in 1835 and occupied by the Selby and Watkins families, and returned to John Brewer's son, Nicholas in 1863 for $4500. The house was sold to Capt. Charles Slayton in 1923. The Slayton House was left to the Historic Annapolis Foundation in 1992 by Morgan Slayton and used as their Designer Showhouse in 1997.

The John Ridout House. 120 Duke of Gloucester Street. Built 1765 for John Ridout, secretary to Governor Horatio Sharp. George and Martha Washington were entertained here. John Ridout was an Oxford graduate who came to Annapolis in 1753. Later married Mary Ogle.

Governor's Mansion. State Circle. Land was purchased in 1868 on Church Circle for a new governor's mansion. Until that time there had been several other buildings used. In 1733 the General Assembly had authorized the purchase of land for a mansion, but it was not until 1742 under Gov. Thomas Bladen that 4 acres was purchased near college Creek. This house was never completed and Bladen's Folly is now McDowell Hall on the St. John's campus.

Jennings House was leased by Gov. Horatio Sharpe, and in 1769 the property was purchased by Gov. Robert Eden, the last provincial governor. When he left for England the house was confiscated by the state and used as the governor's residence for 90 years. Jennings House was conveyed to the US Naval Academy in 1868.

The present house was built in 1870 and Gov. Oden Bowie was the first governor to live in it. The house was remodeled 1935-36, with further renovations in 1947. The skylight was installed in 1987 and in 1990 the fountain placed in the garden. Government House is administered by the Government House Trust.

Hammond-Harwood House. 21 Maryland Avenue. Designed by William Buckland for the bride-to-be of Mathias Hammond 1774. She thought he loved

64

the house and furnishings more than her and eloped with another man. Mr. Hammond never lived in the house, nor married, but maintained the house as an office. The house was sold in 1811 to Chief Justice Jeremiah Townley Chase who gave it to his daughter Francis when she married Richard Lockerman. Their daughter married William Harwood, great grandson of William Buckland. The last family occupant was Hester Ann Harwood who died in 1924. St. John's College purchased the house at auction in 1926. It was closed until 1938 when the Maryland Garden Club rented it. The house was not wired for electricity until the 1940's. Friends of the house restored and furnished this historic home. It has tobacco motifs, as the family's fortune was made in the tobacco trade.

Whitehall. Built 1764 for Governor Horatio Sharp. Overlooking Whitehall Creek. Beautiful Palladian house.

Charles Carroll House. 107 Duke of Gloucester Street. Additions of house built for Charles Carroll of Carrollton (1737-1832) in 1735, only Catholic signer of the Declaration of Independence, and one of Maryland's first Senators.. Part of original house built 1690's for Charles Carroll the Settler. At the time of Charles Carroll the Settler's death in 1720 he owned 47,777 acres of land in Maryland and one-quarter of Annapolis. Gardens overlook Spa Creek. OTP

Upton Scott House. Shipwright Street. Dr. Upton Scott was born in Ireland, trained in medicine in Scotland, and built this house in 1762. Gov. Eden died in the house in 1784. Francis Scott Key lived here while a student at St. John's College. The house was acquired by the School Sisters of Notre Dame in 1876 and used as convent until 1968. Restored by Mr. and Mrs. Coleman DuPont. Now a private home.

Callahan House. 164 Conduit Street. Built c 1780 at the corner of College Avenue and Bladen Street for John Callahan, Commissioner of the Land Office. The house was sold by his widow Sarah Buckland Callahan to Summerville Pinkney in 1803. In 1900 the house was moved to St. John's Street when the Court of Appeals building was constructed 1903 and demolished in 1972. The house was then used as a dormitory for St. John's College. The house was moved to its present site in 1972 and became the property of the city.

Ogle Hall. 251 King George Street. Built 1735 by Dr. William Stevenson who died in 1739. The house was rented to Gov. Samuel Ogle and his wife Ann Tasker Ogle. Governor Ogle introduced horse racing to the state and organized the Jockey Club in 1743. In 1753 the house was sold to Col. Benjamin Tasker, Jr. brother of Mrs. Ogle. He sold the property to her in 1760, and in 1773 she sold it to her son Benjamin. Benjamin Ogle was Governor of Maryland 1798-1801. General Lafayette planted a yew tree in the garden during his last trip to the U.S., and was made an honorary citizen of Maryland. In 1839 the house was sold to Mrs. Edward Lloyd V, whose daughter had married Franklin Buchanan in 1835. He was the first Superintendent of the Naval Academy 1845, and during the Civil War became the first admiral in the Confederate Navy. The house is now the Naval Academy Alumni Association.

Acton House at Acton Place and Franklin Streets is located on the first tract of land granted in Annapolis with a patent in 1657 to Richard Patent. This lovely location on spa Creek now is home to the main house of what was once a tobacco plantation built by Philip Hammond in 1760. Mathias Hammond, youngest son of Philip, was to build the Hammond-Harwood House.

Masonic Lodge. 162 Conduit Street. In 1998 Masonic Lodge 89 celebrates its 150th Anniversary. The Masons were the builders of cathedrals and churches using stone, and it is fit that they now occupy a magnificent building. The Lloyd Dulany House was built c 1771 for Lloyd Dulany who had inherited his wealth from his mother, and built this very expensive, once elaborately furnished house. During the American Revolution his property was confiscated for his Tory beliefs. Mr. Dulany was killed in a duel in London in 1782 by the former rector of St. Anne's Church, Bennett Allen. The property eventually became part of Mann's Tavern.

Best Colonial and 19th Century Buildings

Jonas Green House. 124 Charles Street. 410-263-5892. This wonderful house dates from the 1690's and is one of Annapolis' oldest residences. It was home to Jonas Green from 1738-1767, and is still occupied by members of the Green family. Jonas Green was a cousin of Benjamin Franklin's, and like him founded a newspaper "The Maryland Gazette". He was also a licensed printer for the Maryland Colonial Legislature and printed early American currency. Several members of the Green family married into the Harwood family of the Hammond-Harwood house.

Shiplap House. 18 Pinkney Street. Built 1713 on lot owned by Benjamin Tasker. Later used by Edward Smith as a residence and inn. In the 1780's John Humphrey rented it as the "Sign of the Harp and Crown" tavern. It was eventually a rooming house with 27 people living there, and later condemned by the city, but was rescued by the Historic Annapolis Foundation, which now uses it for its offices. The building has 3 types of overlapping wood siding, similar to a ship. Frank B. Mayer, an artist, lived and worked here.

<u>Maritime Museum</u>. 77 Main Street. During the Revolutionary War this was used by victualling officers to store supplies for Continental Army and Navy. Restored 18th c warehouse. Now part of Historic Annapolis Foundation.

<u>Reynolds Tavern</u>. 7 Church Circle. 410-626-0381. In 1747 William Reynolds, a hatter and dry goods salesman, leased this building from St. Anne's Church. He not only sold hats, but rented rooms and ran an "ordinary which served hot and cold food and liquor to visitors." It was then known as "The Beaver and Lac d'Hat". The Reynolds family maintained the tavern until 1796 when it was sold to John Davidson. His widow was to run a boarding house here until 1811 when it was sold to Farmers National Bank. A fuel company wanted to buy the property in 1936 and tear down the building, but it was saved by a group of Annapolitans with funds from the Female Orphan Society, and converted into the Annapolis Library. The library outgrew the site in 1974 when the building was transferred to the National Trust for Historic Preservation, which then leased it to the Historic Annapolis Foundation. Today it once again serves fine meals and drink.

<u>Middleton Tavern</u>. Market Place. Built c 1750, and owned by Elizabeth Bennett who sold it to Horatio Middleton in 1750. He also ran a sailing ferry to the Eastern Shore. The building was purchased in the 1780's by John Randall. For a while it was Mandie's Confectionary. Fire gutted the building in 1971 and 1973.

<u>Peggy Stewart House</u>. 207 Hanover Street. The house was built in 1761-64 by Thomas Rutland. In 1772 Daniel of St. Thomas Jenifer bought the house. During the Revolution the house was owned by Anthony Stewart, a merchant, who had imported tea, and set fire to his brig "The Peggy Stewart" for Annapolis' own tea party. It was then bought again by Mr. Jenifer and then sold to Thomas Stone, Signer of the Declaration of Independence, in 1779. In 1783 the house was sold to Thomas Harwood, Treasurer of the Western Shore. His son, Gen. Richard Harwood inherited the house, living there with his wife, Sarah Callahan, granddaughter of William Buckland. Now private residence.

<u>Windsor House.</u> C 1760. Built for Reverdy Johnson on North West Street and now on College Green off St. John's Street.

<u>Edward Smith House</u>. Pinkney Street. Built 1713 for innkeeper Edward Smith. Fine example of 3 story wooden house.

<u>McDowell House</u>. St. John's College. Started by Thomas Bladen 1742 as the governor's mansion. The Assembly withdrew the funds as they thought it was too "extravagant". Completed 1784.

Customs House. 99 Main Street. Built 1770's and used for baking bread for Revolutionary War troops. Burned 1790, reconstructed 1792. Later grocery store. Now Sign O' the Whale.

139 Market Street. May have been built by Charles Carroll the Settler. Later owned by Thomas Larkin who sold it to the Hon. Henry Plater, a tobacco farmer and Secretary to Baltimore's Council. Philanthropist Paul Mellon bought the house in 1941 and presented it to St. John's College, his alma mater, for the President's House. It was later sold and is privately owned.

Adams Kilty House. 131 Charles Street. William Kilty was an attorney who published Kilty's Laws of Maryland. Lovely freestanding brick home. Privately owned.

Donaldson-Steuart House. 10 Francis Street. This is one of the earliest brick houses in Annapolis c 1730's and is built on land Gov. Nicholson had given for a free school. Henry Donaldson was a town merchant. The house was later leased to Dr. George Steuart and then sublet to Isaac McHard for the "Sign of the Indian King" in 1773.

Workman House. 10 Francis Street. This house was built for Anthony Workman who came Annapolis as an indentured servant and made a fortune in smuggling. The house was built as a tavern on King William School land.

211-213 Main Street. Old City Hall and Engine House 1821-22.

House by the "Town Gates". 63 West Street. A federal home with gabled roof built c1830's at the site of the original town gates.

Artisan's House. 43 Pinkney Street. C 1777

Dulaney-Duvall House. 179 Duke of Gloucester Street. Built 1730. Was winter home for Nicholas Worthington, a plantation owner.

170 Duke of Gloucester Street. Originally the Forensic Club. Now B&B

Sands House. 130 Prince George Street. Built 1680 and is oldest standing frame residence in Annapolis built for Richard Hill. He and Robert Proctor owned the land in 1685 that comprised Annapolis. Robert Proctor is thought to have had a tavern near the site of St. Mary's Church.

Bordley-Randall House. State Circle. Built by Thomas Bordley c 1717. In 1847 purchased by Alexander Randall, a prominent attorney. In 1947 P.V.H.

Weems, developer of the Weems (celestial) system of navigation, purchased the house.

The Little Brice House. 195 Prince George Street. Owned by Amos Garrett, first mayor of Annapolis and sold to John Brice II in 1737.

Brooksby-Shaw House. State Circle. Built 1720's for Cornelius Brooksby. Later owned by prominent cabinet maker John Shaw. Now State offices.

Patrick Creagh House/ Aunt Lucy's Bake Shop. 160 Prince George Street. Built 1735-47 for Patrick Creagh, born on the Eastern Shore c 1697. He was a shipbuilder, whose boatworks were at the foot of Prince George Street and later the site of the colony jail or "gaol". He was also a painter, ship owner, tobacco trader, slave trader and contractor who built the "Old Treasury". He was later to purchase a 500 acre farm on the South River and 120 acres on Dorsey Creek, "Chance on Curtis Creek, thirty-three acres near Beard's Creek and 80 acres on Acton Creek. His daughter married Richard MacCubbin, a merchant.

Sometime around 1800 Lucy and John Smith, a free black couple, became tenants on the property, operating a carriage and carting business. His wife, Aunt Lucy, operated a bake shop near the corner of Main and Green Street. They were later to purchase the property and the house is still called "Aunt Lucy's Bake Shop".

The old rectory of St. Anne's Church. 215-217 Hanover Street. Built 1760. Later owned by Philip Key, great-grandfather of Francis Scott Key who sold the land to the Episcopal Church in 1759, who maintained it as a rectory until 1885.

Retallick-Brewer House. 183 Green Street. In 1718 the lot was surveyed for Amos Garrett, a merchant and first Mayor of Annapolis. He died in 1727 leaving the property to four heirs who conveyed the property to Dr. Charles Carroll in 1735. The house was leased to Simon Retallick in 1788. He was a blacksmith and ironmaster, and put the iron bars on the Old Treasury Building. In 1820 the house was sold to Elizabeth Retallick Rawlings, who left the house to her daughter, Eliza Ann Brewer.

26 West Street. In the 18c Mrs. Ghiselin's Ordinary was an inn. Thomas Jefferson and James Monroe are known to have stayed here in 1784 as delegates from Virginia to the Continental Congress. In 1965 it became the Capital City Federal Savings and Loan Association.

Lockerman-Tilton House. 9 Maryland Avenue. c1740. This house has been owned by John Rogers, first chancellor of the State of Maryland, and Josephine Tilton. Her husband accompanied Adm. Perry to Japan. The kitchen was a separate house and was once home to Comm. Gordon Ellyson, the Navy's first aviator.

18 West Street. Lovely brick building. Built c 1790 for Allen Quynn, a former mayor of Annapolis. Now offices of Parrott & Donahue and Miles & Stockbridge, Attorneys at Law.

Farmers National Bank. Church Circle. Built 1805

162 Conduit Street and Duke of Gloucester Streets. Large 18th c house. Once home of Thomas Dulany, a Tory. (See above) Later bought by George Mann for use as an inn and tavern. The colorful homes along this block of Conduit Street were also part of the Inn. They became private residences in 1912. Known as Mann's City Hotel a ball was held following George Washington's resignation 1783. The Maryland Society of the Cincinnati was founded here. Mann's Tavern later became the City Hotel. This was destroyed by fire in 1917.

Annapolis Summer Garden Theatre. 27 Compromise Street. Once was the Shaw Blacksmith Shop

Tobacco Prise House. 4 Pinkney Street. Tobacco warehouse, shipped in hogshead barrels.

Waterwitch Hook and Ladder Company. 33 East Street. Built 1913

City Dock. Has been in use since 1650 as dock. Thomas Todd had a boatyard here. The Ship Carpenter's lot was to the left of City Dock. Once site of skipjacks, bugeyes, and other vessels, and many old wooden docks.

The Market Place is the fifth built on the site, the present one in 1858. A site was selected as early as 1684, but no building existed. In 1717 the first Market House opened on State Circle. In 1784 filled land on the dock was deeded by eight Annapolis residents for use as a market, which is still maintained. Records show the market master was also the town lamplighter. The lamp finials were in the shape of tobacco leaves.

Maryland Inn. Church Circle at Duke of Gloucester Street. This was once called Drummer's Lot. The town crier brought together the towns' people with the roll of drums to read official proclamations. In 1718 the lot was owned by Philemon Lloyd, grandfather of Molly Chew who was to marry William Paca in

1763. The inn was built in 1772 by Thomas Hyde of Severn. Now part of Historic Inns of Annapolis.

Benson-Hammond House. West Street. 19th c farmhouse built by Thomas Benson. Now Anne Arundel County Historical Society.

The Barracks. 43 Pinkney Street. 410-269-1737. Furnished to look like Revolutionary War barracks. Open by appointment

Gassaway Feldmeyer House. 194 Prince George Street, Built 1878-80 for Augustus Gassaway, a Mayor of Annapolis, postmaster, and secretary to the Maryland Senate. After his sudden death in 1880 the house was willed to his daughter. The Gassaway family had settled in Annapolis in 1650. The house was purchased by the Feldmeyer family in 1903. The house is Italianate in architecture.

Merchand-Dorsey House. 211 Prince George Street. This c1700 home was built for Major Edward Dorsey. The first Annapolis meeting of the Maryland Assembly was held here February 28, 1695.

Golder House. 42-50 West Street. A Mr. Golder had a store here called the "Sign of the Waggon and horse." He died in 1765 from eating poisonous mushrooms.

Price House. 230-236 Main Street. Constructed 1821-1832 by Henry Price, a "free man of color" and lay minister at the Annapolis Station Methodist Episcopal Church. He was one of the founders of Asbury United Methodist Church on West Street.

Stick Style Houses

138 Conduit Street. The Zimmerman House. Built for a conductor of the Navy Band.

Schools

The Annapolis Elementary School on Green Street was the first school to be integrated in Anne Arundel County.

St. Mary's Parochial School building on Duke of Gloucester Street was erected in 1880. St. Mary's had a school for white students and another for colored students 1903-1949.

The Stanton School at 92 West Washington Street is currently being reconditioned to serve as the Stanton Center. The school was named for Secretary of War Edwin Stanton, a supporter of the abolitionist cause. It was built in 1900. However, the school had been founded in Parole between 1867-68. The present property was bought in 1869 for the "colored children of the City of Annapolis and its vicinity". Up until that time black children were educated at St. Mary's and the Gallilean Fisherman School. In 1917 the building also became the first high school for blacks. When Bates High School was opened Stanton continued as an elementary school, and in 1938 became Bates Junior High School. The building will now become a community center.

Bates School was named for Wiley H. Bates who came to Annapolis from North Carolina in the late 1870's. He was a coal merchant and store keeper, and served as an alderman in the Annapolis City Council 1897-99. He bequeathed a sum of money for the school. The school was built in 1932 as Bates High School.

Maryland Hall for the Performing Arts was once the Annapolis high School.

Churches

St. Anne's Episcopal Church. Church Circle. Was one of 30 parishes created in 1692 by the General Assembly when it made the Church of England the Established Church of Maryland. The church served as the Chapel Royal until 1715 when the province was returned to Lord Baltimore. Taxes (paid in tobacco) were imposed on all inhabitants to maintain buildings and the clergy who were chosen by governmental authority. The first church was erected 1692 with pews set aside for the Governor and legislators. King William sent over his silver communion service, which is still used today.

The church was torn down in 1775, losing state support in 1776. The bricks and other building material for the church were used in the Revolutionary War. The second church was built in 1792, and consecrated by Bishop Thomas Claggett, an ancestor of the author of this book. The architect was Joseph Horatio Anderson, architect also of the present State House. Fire gutted this church in 1858.

72

The present church was built in 1859 in Romanesque Revival style. The steeple was delayed due to the Civil War and finished in 1866. The Bishop of Maryland and the rector of St. Anne's were opposed to secession, the congregation pro-confederate. The town clock is in the steeple, which rings every fifteen minutes. Some of the stained windows are by Tiffany. The reredos was carved in Oberammergau, Germany in 1920. The memorial window by Tiffany was exhibited at the Columbian Exposition in Chicago in 1893. The old organ was manufactured by the Moller Organ Co. and cost $21,000 in 1945, and was replaced in 1975 with one produced in Freiburg, Germany. Parish records date from 1705 and include the bequest of a Bible from Major General John Hammond in 1710 and a Prayer Book purchased in 1764 with the prayer to King George III inked out and replaced with one for the President of the United States. The brass eagle lectern is in memory of Captain James Wadell, commander of the Confederate Raider "Shenandoah".

Buried in the churchyard:
Amos Garrett, first Mayor of Annapolis, died 1728
Nicholas Greenbury, aided Gov. Nicholson in laying out Annapolis, died 1697
Benjamin Tasker, Acting Governor 1752-53, died 1768
Sir Robert Eden, last colonial Governor of Maryland, died 1784
Major General John Hammond, great-grandfather of Mathias Hammond, died 1737
Daniel Dulany, the Elder, wrote "The Rights of the Inhabitants of Maryland to the Benefit of English Law".
Carroll Tomb - contains the remains of Dr. Charles Carroll, John Henry Carroll, Charles Carroll the Barrister and Margaret Tilghman Carroll, widow of the Barrister.
Bordley Tomb - Margaret Chew Bordley, first wife of John Beale Bordley, who was raised by her stepfather Daniel Dulany the Elder of Annapolis, following the death of her father Samuel Chew. Her mother was a granddaughter of Col. Edward Lloyd of Talbot County. Her sister, Ann Mary Chew was the first wife of William Paca. In 1790 a bequest of land on College Creek was given by Elizabeth Bordley for the St. Anne's Cemetery.

St. Mary's Church. Duke of Gloucester Street. Prior to 1858 Jesuit priests had come from St. Mary's to visit the Roman Catholic population. The present church was erected 1859 on land given by Mrs. John McTavish and her three sisters, all grand-daughters of Charles Carroll of Carrollton who was the original owner of the property. Also on the property is the Upton Scott House. Dr. Scott was born in Ireland and came to Annapolis in 1753 with Governor Horatio Sharp and became his physician. The house was built in 1765. Dr. Scott remained a Loyalist during the Revolution. His wife was Elizabeth Ross

Key, whose nephew, Francis Scott Key, lived with them while attending St. John's College.

Presbyterian Church. Corner of Duke of Gloucester and Conduit Streets. Built 1846 on the site of a theater.

Mt. Moriah A.M.E. Church. Franklin Street. During the 1800's the church was an African Methodist Episcopal Church, which had been founded in 1799. It was one of the first U.S. churches built by free blacks. Now Bannecker-Douglas Museum.

Calvary Methodist Church. Was also known as Maryland Avenue Methodist Episcopal Church. The church was organized in 1785, and the church built 1859. The building was offered for sale in 1940 for $17,500. It was leased to the USO in 1941 for an entertainment center for servicemen. When that moved out in 1942 it was leased to First Church of Christ Scientist, who bought it for $14,000 in 1944. It was recently sold again.

183 Duke of Gloucester Street. Site of first Synagogue in Annapolis, Kneseth Israel, which was chartered in 1906 and the home purchased in 1910. Used until 1912, and moved to site on Prince George Street. Now at 1152 Spa Road.

Asbury Methodist Church. 1888 American Gothic. Once home of early African American congregation.

Historic Cemeteries

St. Anne's. The first mayor of Annapolis, Amos Garrett, is buried here.

St. Mary's - Many of the Redemptorists and Priests of St. Mary's buried here. St. Justin (martyred 308-318?) was interred here in 1989.

Annapolis National Cemetery. West Street and Taylor Avenue

Luther Palmer Memorial Cemetery. Riva Road and West Street. This was the burial ground for the Edwards Chapel Methodist Episcopal Church South, and is over 100 years old (1897). The church stood where the Econo Lodge now is. Mr. Palmer deeded the land to the church in 1897 for $5.00, and was first called edwards Chapel Cemetery. About 150 people are buried on the site.

Brewer Hill Cemetery. 800 West Street. Historic cemetery and for many years the only cemetery for Blacks in Annapolis. The property was recently restored.

Residences of Famous People

Peggy Stewart House. 207 Hanover Street. Home of Thomas Stone,who drafted the Article of Confederation, Signer of the Declaration of Independence and later U.S. Senator. Built by Anthony Stewart, who in 1774 was forced to burn the brig, Peggy Stewart, because of tea and other goods from England on board. The property was sold to Thomas Stone in 1779.

William Pinkney House located across from the Jonas Greene House on Charles Street was home to William Pinkney whom Daniel Webster declared was the "greatest of advocates".

Maryland Historical Trust. 21 State Circle. Built c 1720 with a gambrel roof for a coach maker. From 1784-1829 shop of John Shaw, the noted Annapolis cabinet maker who made the furniture for the Old Senate chambers.

Ogle Hall. 247 King George Street. Built 1739. Home of Governor Samuel Ogle. Now restored by the Naval Academy Alumni Association for headquarters.

Zimmerman House. 133 Conduit Street. Built c 1895. Once residence for Charles Zimmerman, Naval Academy bandmaster.

William Paca House. 194 Prince George Street. Colonial legislator, Signer of Declaration of Independence, Governor of Maryland for three terms, later federal judge.

Chase-Lloyd House. 22 Maryland Avenue. Samuel Chase was a Signer of Declaration of Independence, state legislator, served as Judge on Supreme Court.

Charles Carroll House. 107 Duke of Gloucester Street. Signer of Declaration of Independence, state senator, U.S. Senator.

230-236 Main Street. In 1763 the painter, Charles Wilson Peale moved his business here. He had been born on the Eastern Shore, but his father died at an early age leaving his mother with five young children. John Beale Bordley helped her move to Annapolis where Peale became a saddler's apprentice. Bordley was later to become William Paca's brother-in-law. Peale was to study painting under John Hesselius of Annapolis. But it was John Singleton Copley's tutelage in Boston that eventually permitted him to study in England under Benjamin West.

21 State Circle. John Shaw, the noted cabinet maker moved to Annapolis from Glasgow, Scotland in 1745. He designed the thirteen starred flag, each with eight points, was on the vestry of St. Anne's Church, and was the keeper of the town's fire engine.

Bordley - Randall House. State Circle. Birthplace of Reverdy Johnson, Attorney General of the United States under Zachary Taylor, and later American minister (ambassador) to England.

St. John's College

St. John's College was founded in 1696 as King William's School at a site on State Circle and through the State Charter of 1784 located in "Bladen's Folly". The College had continuous financial problems right from the start. During the Civil War the property was used as a camp and hospital, but became a college again in 1866. From 1884-1923 it was a military academy. In 1937 Stringfellow Barr and Scott Buchanan rescued the college and initiated the curriculum which is centered around 100 Great Books. It is the third oldest college in the U.S. behind Harvard and William and Mary.

Famous people who attended the college are two nephews of George Washington, sent by him, Fairfax (1794) and Laurence (1798) Washington; Mrs. Washington's grandson George Washington Park Custis; Alexander Randall, Governor of Liberia; Charles S. Winder, Brig. Gen. in the Confederate Army; John Shaw, son of the cabinetmaker and a good friend of Francis Scott Key, became a noted doctor and poet; and Francis Scott Key, author of "The Star Spangled Banner" who graduated in 1796 and founded the St. John's Alumni Association. William Pinkney was a delegate to the Constitutional Convention in 1788, ambassador to England and Russia and U.S. Senator. Many of the rectors at St. Anne's Church were also principals (presidents) of St. John's College. Women were not admitted until 1951.

McDowell House. Named for first president of the college. Once was called "Bladen's Folly" for the expense needed to complete what was to be the governor's mansion, and later denied moneys to complete the project.

Charles Carroll the Barrister House. Once located at Main and Conduit Streets, moved 1955. Now Admissions and Alumni Office. Dr. Carroll was the author of the Maryland Bill of Rights. Dr. Charles Carroll the Barrister married Margaret Tilghman. They had no heirs and the property was left to a nephew Nicholas Maccubbin stipulating he must change his name to Carroll and use the family coat of arms.

76

<u>Dr. Bray's Library</u> was the first public library in Maryland with books supplied by Princess Anne of England in 1699. These are now in the House of Records. Students at St. John's study only from 100 Great Books and the faculty must be able to teach from any of them.

<u>Mitchell Art Gallery</u>. Excellent exhibitions. Named for wife of Carlton Mitchell, mentioned in Yachting chapter.

<u>French Monument</u>. Dedicated to the French soldiers who served in the American Revolution, that were encamped on the St. John's campus. The monument came about through the inspiration of Naval Academy professor, Henry Marion, who was serving in Cherbourg, France, when the body of John Paul Jones was removed from France, and brought to the Naval Academy. The monument was dedicated April 11,1911, presided over by President Howard Taft and Ambassador Jean Jules Jusserand of France.

<u>The Liberty Tree</u> in front of Woodward Hall is over 400 years old.

Nearby Great Homes and Small Treasures

<u>London Town Public House</u>. Londontown Road, Edgewater. 410-222-1919. The name first appears in records of 1684. From 1689-95 the Anne Arundel County Court met here. The Georgian colonial house was completed in 1764 by William Brown, though artifacts on property date back to the 1600's. Much archeological work is being done on the property. The publick house was on the north-south "Tobacco Road", the main road between Philadelphia and Richmond. The port contained about 100 buildings. Mr. Brown was a cabinet maker and licensed to run the ferry from London town to Annapolis. During the dig here the first use of Delft china in the U.S. was discovered. In 1996 George Rumney's Tavern, which operated 1690-1775, was located. The physician Richard Hill grew Jerusalem Oak, now known as lamb's-quarters, which was believed to cure depression. The colony died out for unknown reasons, perhaps the silting of the river or the insolvency of Mr. Brown? The lovely home was built with slave labor, and later was the Anne Arundel County Almshouse. The property is situated on 23 acres with extensive archeological and restoration work now going on.

<u>Whitehall.</u> Whitehall Road, off Route 50. This elegant mansion on Whitehall Creek was built by Gov. Horatio Sharp 1764-65 as a summer retreat and most likely was designed by Matthew Buckland. Gov. Sharp willed his estate to John Ridout, his former secretary and friend.

South River Club - near London Town, was built c1740 and is thought to be first social club in continuous use. The men's social club meets four times a year for dinner.

Sotterley. Once on 4,000 acre grant given to Captain Thomas Cornwallis on Patuxent River. It was named "Resurrection Manor". In 1710 the property was subdivided and 890 acres purchased by James Bowles. He began construction of the main house, but died 1727. His widow married George Plater II who with his son George Plater III completed the house, naming it after the ancestral home in Suffolk, England. George Plater III represented Maryland at the Continental Congress and served as president of the state convention that ratified the Constitution, and was a member of the electoral college that elected Gen. Washington president. Mr. Plater was elected Governor of Maryland in 1791. The house and grounds are OTP and run by the Sotterly Mansion Foundation. Beautiful gardens. Land sloping down to Patuxent.

Wye Plantation. Home of Edward Lloyd V. The abolitionist and writer Frederick Douglas worked here as a slave until he was 21, and then fled to Philadelphia where he became a free black.

Doughhoregan – The Carroll family country home, is located on Manor Lane, Ellicott City on Patuxent River. The name is Gaelic for "House of Kings". The house was built in 1717 on 15,000 acres. Charles Carroll of Carrollton is buried here. Still in Carroll family.

Special Buildings

The Maryland State Law Library. Courts of Appeal Building. 361 Rowe Blvd. 410-974-3395. The Library was established by the State Legislature in 1826, and now has about 300,000 volumes. These include records and briefs of appellate court cases, Maryland legislative history, Maryland State Bar Association Ethics Opinions, Superceded Maryland Codes, Maryland history, the Maryland Women's Hall of Fame, and special collections such as John James Audobon's "Birds of America".

Restoration of old Buildings in Process or Recently Completed (1997-98)

Maynard-Burgess House - Duke of Gloucester Street. Once owned by John Maynard, a free black man, who worked as a waiter and bought the building in

1847 for $400. It remained in the possession of black families until 1990, and is now being restored. Built c 1780.

Manressa - built 1926 as a retreat house for Catholic men. Now extended care facility.

Slayton House - used as Showhouse for Historic Annapolis Foundation Spring 1997. This building is to be sold by the Foundation. Extensive archeological work has done on the premises, but the house itself needs extensive and loving work.

Court House. Church Circle. New addition opened 1997

Most Beautiful Gardens and Other Special Nature Enclaves

Many of the private homes in downtown Annapols have beautiful gardens. These are not open to the public, but some may be viewed from the street. Among the author's favorites are those listed here.

William Paca House. 1 Martin Street. 2 acres of restored formal gardens with gravel walks, topiary, greenhouse. Beautiful all year round.
Hammond-Harwood House. 19 Maryland Avenue
Helen Avalynne Tawes Gardens. Rowe Blvd. and Taylor Avenue. Named for former First Lady of Maryland
Chase-Lloyd House. 22 Maryland Avenue
Superintendent's House. Naval Academy
St. Mary's Church. Duke of Gloucester Street
All four corner homes at Maryland Avenue and King George Street
Arboretum of London Town Public House. Londontown Road, Edgewater. 18th c inn on South River. 8 acres of gardens.
Blue Heron Center at Quiet Waters Park
Smithsonian Institution for Environmental Studies. Old Muddy Creek Road. Tours.
Southgate Memorial Fountain. Church Circle. Dedicated to William Scott Southgate, former rector of St. Anne's Church who had worked within the Annapolis community, particularly African Americans.
Park about halfway down Fleet Street.
40 Cornhill Street.
Upton Scott House. Shipwright Street

Fine Brick Buildings

Annapolis is noted for its fine brick buildings, and may have more of these than most of America's other historic towns and cities. Examples of architecturally elegant brick homes can be found on Maryland Avenue, Duke of Gloucester, Charles, Conduit, Prince and Franklin Streets. One particularly lovely brick home, at the corner of Conduit and Duke of Gloucester Streets, 179 Duke of Gloucester, had part of the building removed when Conduit was extended to the water. Previously it had only gone from Main to Duke of Gloucester. London Town in Edgewater is also a noted brick structure.

Brick churches - Almost all of the churches downtown are brick and include St. Anne's, St. Mary's, and the Presbyterian Church.

Brick public buildings - State House, Post Office and other government offices; many shops along Main Street.

Most Beautiful or Unusual Doorways of Homes

Hammond-Harwood House. Maryland Avenue
Chase-Lloyd House. Maryland Avenue
11 College Street. Angels with trumpets
194, 201, 203, 211 Prince George Street
60 Cornhill Street
Ridout House and Ridout Row. Duke of Gloucester Street
162, 164 Conduit Street
139, 141 Market Street
179 Duke of Gloucester Street
St. Anne's Parish. Duke of Gloucester Street

Favorite Weathervanes

St. Anne's Church. Church Circle
The State House. State Circle
Flower Box. College and King George Streets
United States Post Office. Church Circle
Legislative Services Building. In front of Capital
Louis Goldstein Legislative Building. Calvert Street

Places with Best Views

Top of Main Street looking down from St. Anne's Church

Homes along Severn River, Spa Creek and Bay Ridge
Houses on Revell, Compromise and Shipwright Streets

Special Sites

Bloomsbury Square - Located at College and Bladen Streets, this square was named for Bloomsbury Square in London, around which lived many well-to-do families such as the Lords Baltimore, who obtained information on the new colony of Maryland. The Square was set out by Governor Francis Nicholson in 1695. The property was first owned by Charles Carroll (1660-1720), grandfather of Charles Carroll of Carrollton, the only Catholic signer of the Declaration of Independence; and William Bladen (1670-1718), a lawyer and owner of printing presses, and father of Thomas Bladen (1698-1780), Governor of Maryland.

The north side of the square was a shipyard and the largest vessel for carrying tobacco was launched from here in 1747, the "Rumney and Long". The area was also where free Blacks lived.

Today it is the site of some lovely brick state government office buildings - William S. James Senate Office Building, Income Tax Building, Louis Goldstein Treasury Building, and the Thomas Lowe House of Delegates Building.

Across the street from this lies State House Square, behind which is the State Capital. State House Square was named on the 200th anniversary of the Court of Appeals in 1978. The Court first convened in 1780 in the Revenue Office on Duke of Gloucester Street. Now it meets in a new building on Rowe Boulevard. In 1976 this office building was replaced to the left by the Legislative Offices Buildings, which has some of the lovely old woodwork and Tiffany windows from the previous building. The statue of Thurgood Marshall is in the center of the square.

World War II Memorial. Pendennis Mount on north side of Naval Academy Bridge. This memorial was dedicated July 23, 1998 to those 6,454 Marylanders who lost their lives during World War II. Senator Robert Dole and four governors of Maryland were present. The memorial was designed by Secundino Fernandez of New York and cost $3 million.

81

Interesting Street and Place Names

Most streets in Annapolis are labeled with their original "Formerly" names. Favorite streets are Duke of Gloucester, Prince George and Cornhill. In August 1948 the Annapolis and Anne Arundel County Chamber of Commerce recommended Duke of Gloucester and Main Streets become one way streets.

Market Street received its name because the wharf at the end was used to bring produce to the market at what is now Market and Duke of Gloucester Streets.

State Circle was once known as Public Circle.

Slippery Hill was the name given to the hill above Spa Creek along Revell, Conduit and Market Streets.

The area near Main and Compromise Streets was the warehouse district, much of it destroyed by fire in 1790. This was rebuilt with store fronts. At the time of the Revolution 77 Main Street was the site of Daniel Dulany's warehouse, and was confiscated due to his allegiance as a Tory. This was used as a victualling warehouse for the troops. During the 19th c 77-79 Main was a dry goods store run by George and John Barber who also ran a steam packet to Baltimore. In the middle of the block Jacob Slemaker made hats. (Hats in the Belfry is now nearby). 99 Main Street was a bakery run by Frederick Grammer who supplied the Continental Army with baked goods during the Revolution.

Fortifications during the Civil War were along Jefferson Street - College to Spa Creeks.

The Washington, Baltimore and Annapolis Railroad Depot was once located at West and Washington Streets, and had a line to the Naval Academy.

West Street was once the only thoroughfare leading off the Annapolis peninsula. It had a palisade with moat and gate erected in 1696. In the 1950's this was the "shopping center" for Annapolis, until Main Street took over about 1970, plus the addition of nearby shopping malls. Much of the street from Taylor Avenue into Church Circle is being revitalized. Several historic buildings have been renovated and at least one large office complex is planned.

Compromise Street was built from filled land on Spa Creek in the 19th c. The street received its name from the compromise of the commissioners to name the street in 1838. The end of Hanover Street was also filled land originally called Governor's Pond.

Fleet Street was named in 1769 by Charles Wallace for the street of the same name in London.

Pinkney Street was once a creek that flowed to the Dock, then silted up and was known as the "Sand Bank". This was to become the Market House, and Annapolis was to become the market town for this region.

Duke of Gloucester Street was named for Queen Anne's only child to live beyond infancy. Prince George Street was named for her husband Prince George of Denmark.

Other interesting street names: Newman was once called Red Head Lane; College Avenue was Tabernacle; West Street, Cowpens Lane; Franklin, Doctor Street; and Main, Church Street - the commercial center of the town.

John Shaw and Archibold Chisholm, prominent cabinet and chair makers had a shop on Church Street during the 1770's.

The shops and post office were on Main Street. All mail had to be picked up and unclaimed mail was listed in The Gazette.

Green Street was laid out by Dr. Charles Carroll in 1752.

The streets also had some interesting rules: There were fines for glass left on property more than 12 hours, letting hogs run wild, for operating a vehicle with wheels less than five inches in width, and for galloping a horse on the street. Animals could not wander at largeon the streets with a bell attached.

Cornhill Street was made up of residences for craftsmen and shopkeepers. Cornhill and Fleet Streets were used by the early governors for gardens and vineyards, and it is thought Governor Nicholson had a home located here. The Bordley family owned the property from 1718-69 when it was purchased by Charles Wallace. The land was leased to tradesmen for 99 years.

37-39 Cornhill was used by John Brewer as a tavern and dry goods store. Thomas Jefferson purchased "gloves, silk stockings, and salt". It is known William Monroe, a carpenter, owned 49 Cornhill and Thomas Callahan, a tailor, 53 Cornhill.

For many years a barber shop was located at the corner of Cornhill and Fleet Streets, and George Washington was shaved there on December 23, 1783 before his resignation.

The creeks too had other names: College once was called Dorsey's Creek, Deep Creek and Graveyard Creek; Spa Creek, Todds Creek and Carroll Creek.

The brick sidewalks were called footways with "Kirb stones", and were probably not put in until after 1820.

Almost all old towns had a 'Battery" for the town guns, and Annapolis' was located at the end of Prince George Street.

The 18th c second County Gaol (jail) was located on a lot at West, Cathedral and Dean Streets, and a third one at Randall and Prince George Street. During the 18th c prisoners were fed 1 pint of corn per day, and 2 pounds of meat per week. The town had gallows for convicted criminals.

The first department store was founded in 1899. Gottleib's was located at 184-186 Main Street.

After the incorporation of Annapolis a license was needed to run a tavern costing 6 pounds per year, and also for selling spirituous liquors and billiards. Liquor could not be sold to indentured servants or slaves without the owner's permission.

Ritchie Highway, named for Gov. Ritchie, was the first dual highway in Maryland, and linked Baltimore and Annapolis.

The dock at the end of King George Street was located in a neighborhood called Hell's Kitchen or Hell Point (now part of the Naval Academy beyond Gate 1).

Along West Street lived Philip Syng, a well known Maryland silversmith and William Faris and Abraham Claude, watchmakers.At 42-50 West lived a Mr. Golder who maintained the "Sign of the Waggon and Horse" store until he died in 1765 after eating poisonous mushrooms. Allyn Quynn, shoemaker, vestryman at St. Anne's Church, Mayor and delegate to the General Assembly lived at 21 West Street. The original town gates and a racecourse were just beyond this in the 1700's.

The Three Mile Oak on Generals Highway became famous on December 17, 1783 when General George Washington stood under it, and told the local citizenry he would not be king of the new nation. General Washington was due in Annapolis the next day to resign his commission as commander-in-chief of the Continental Army. The original tree is long since gone, but in 1967 the garden club planted another oak tree.

African American Places of Interest

As mentioned in the Special Sites section and Recently Restored Properties Annapolis has a rich heritage concerning free blacks. Homes along Duke of Gloucester, East, Cornhill, West, Clay, Fleet and Market Streets have many fine examples of private dwellings for this population. Maryland consistently had a large free black population and before the Civil War it numbered about 43%.

Many of these homes have survived to this day. Prominent examples are the Maynard-Burgess House, Duke of Gloucester Street; the Butler House, 148 Duke of Gloucester Street; 115-121 Market Street, and along the above mentioned streets. William H. Butler, Sr. Was a Civil War veteran, real estate developer and served as a City Alderman 1873-75. His son William, Jr. also served as a City Alderman. The Historic Annapolis Foundation has printed an excellent brochure on this. For further information please contact them at 410-267-9619.

The earliest known black to settle in Maryland was a mulatto, Matthias Sousa, who arrived with the Ark and Dove in St. Mary's. He arrived as an indentured servant to Father Andrew White, but after becoming a free man attended the General Assembly of 1642, commanded a Bay vessel and engaged in the fur trade.

Later indentured servants and slaves were brought to the area to work in the tobacco fields, or as skilled craftsmen. Benjamin Banneker was probably one of the most famous free blacks. He was an astronomer, mathematician and helped lay out what eventually became the U.S. capital, Washington, DC. He is remembered at the Banneker-Douglas museum, along with Frederick Douglass who spoke at the Bethel A.M.E. Church, later Mt. Moriah Church, and presently the museum. The importation of slaves into Maryland was forbidden by an act of the Legislature in 1784. Free blacks were permitted to vote in city elections as early as 1799.

A plaque at the State House honors Matthew Henson, a black from Charles County, who traveled to the North Pole with Admiral Peary.

The statue of Thurgood Marshall, the first black justice of the Supreme Court and a Marylander, is in front of the State House.

Alex Haley found that Kunte Kinte had come from Gambia on board ship to Annapolis in 1767. A marker is placed on City Dock to honor him.

Bates High School was built in 1934 when blacks were permitted to receive a high school education in Annapolis. St. John's admitted its first black student in 1948.

Museums and Homes Open to the Public

Some descriptions of the homes listed here as museums are described in more detail in the chapters on Buildings and Places or the Naval Academy.

Naval Academy Museum. Preble Hall, near Gate 3. 410-267-2108

Bannecker-Douglas Museum. 84 Franklin Street. 410-974-2553. Once Mt. Moriah A.M.E. Church. Named for Benjamin Bannecker and Frederick Douglas, prominent Black men.

Barge House Museum. 133 Bay Shore Drive, Eastport. 410-268-1802. This charming small building has an annual doll house show that displays dolls and furniture made by the Richwood Toy Company. This company was founded in Larchmont, New York by Ida Wood. The Wood family moved to Annapolis in 1950, and a factory was set up at The Eastport Marina. Favorite dolls made by the company included Sandra Sue and Cindy Lou. Today Jerry Wood, son of the late founder, owns the Annapolis sailing school and helped found the Annapolis Boat Show. The Barge Museum is headquarters for the Eastport Historical Committee.

Charles Carroll House. 107 Duke of Gloucester Street. 410-269-1737. Charles Carroll of Carrollton, the only Catholic signer of the Declaration of Independence, was born in this house in 1737.

Chase-Lloyd House. 22 Maryland Avenue. 410-263-2723.

Hammond-Harwood House. 19 Maryland Avenue. 410-269-1714. Built 1774 for Mathias Hammond, a legislator and planter. The house was designed by William Buckland, and has some of Annapolis' most beautiful rooms and garden.

Historic Annapolis Foundation. Shiplap House 18 Pinkney Street. 410-267-7619

Historic Annapolis Foundation Museum Store. 77 Main Street. 410-268-5576

London Town House and Gardens. 839 Londontown Road, Edgewater. 410-

222-1919. London Town was once a tobacco port, and was considered as the site of Maryland's capital. The London Town House was built c 1760 by William Brown, a cabinet maker and planter, licensed to run the ferry from London to Annapolis. The town declined in the mid 1700's. Today much archeological work is being done on the property, which has lovely gardens.

William Paca House and Garden. 194 Prince George Street. 410-263-5553. This gracious mansion was built in 1763 by William Paca, a young lawyer for his marriage to Ann Mary Chew. She died in 1771, and in 1774 he married Ann Harrison of Philadelphia. She died in 1780, and several years later the house was sold.

It remained in private hands until 1901 when it was sold to the Annapolis Hotel Corporation. The house became part of the Carvel Hall Hotel. In 1965 its outdated plumbing and style forced the owners to think about selling the complex, which was to be razed for a new office complex. Thanks to the efforts of the Historic Annapolis Foundation who bought the house, and the Maryland Legislature gave funds for the gardens, this magnificent house was saved.

Brice House. 42 East Street. 410-263-5553

Chesapeake Children's Museum. Festival Shopping Center. 2331 D Forest Drive. 410-266-0677

Maryland State Archives, Hall of Records. 350 Rowe Boulevard. 410-974-3867

Maryland State House. State Circle. Tours. 410-974-3611

Davis' Pub

Ginger Doyle

Chapter 8

Eastport

One of the most charming places in Annapolis besides the Historic District lies across Spa Creek. Eastport was once home to a few farms, later watermen - oysters and crabbing, seafood packing, and boat building. During World War II subchasers and PT boats were built for the Navy.

The peninsula (Horn Point) between Spa Creek and Back Creek was first patented in 1665 by Robert Clarkson, a Quaker. A few farms prospered owned by the Ogle, Hill and Barber families. During the Revolutionary War Lafayette's Continental Light Infantry camped on Spa Creek in 1781. A state historical marker is erected at the site. Fort Horn (named for Congressman Van Horn) was built to protect Annapolis during the Revolutionary War, War of 1812 and Civil War.

The first house was built by Henry Medford in 1857. Heller's Boat Yard was established in 1865. In 1868 the area east of Sixth Street (101 acres) was sold to the Mutual Building Association of Annapolis to be subdivided into 265 lots. Black families mainly settled along Back Creek and white along Spa Creek. The first wooden bridge to connect Annapolis and Eastport was constructed in 1868 and replaced by a metal bridge in 1908 on Fourth Street. The area became residential and commercial, especially for tradesmen and watermen.

During the 1920s the Eastport Civic Association was formed to consider a possible merger with Annapolis. Several times Annapolis attempted to annex Eastport. The Spa Creek Bridge was again replaced, this time on Sixth Street with the present structure in 1949. The town was annexed to Annapolis in 1951. The bridge was closed for three weeks in February 1998 for major repairs, the first time since 1949, and Eastporters joyfully proclaimed the "Maritime Republic of Eastport".

Many noted shipyards sprang up along Spa Creek between first and Second Streets. Among these were Chance Construction Company, Annapolis Yacht Yard and later Trumpy's. The Annapolis Yacht Yard built sub chasers and PT boats during World War II. Trumpy's built boats for the Navy during both the Korean and Vietnam wars (see Yachting section). Some of the most beautiful yachts on the Chesapeake and elsewhere came from this famous yard.

Other important boat builders were Mason & Sons (1918-70) who built cabin cruisers, Owens Yacht Company, forerunner of the Owens Yacht Co. in

Dundalk, Lewis's Boatyard (1896-1963) – now the site of the Tecumseh Condominiums on Severn Avenue, Sadler's (1947-80) at Third Street and Spa Creek, and Arnie Gay's at Shipwright and Sixth Streets. At the end of First Street was Heller's Boatyard (1870-1936), now the Yacht Haven complex. Sarles Boatyard dates from 1907 and is still run by the Sarles family.

Other commercial buildings were the Annapolis Glass Company, founded in 1868, which produced glass, china and pottery. Charles Murphy the owner was from Eastport, Maine, thus the present name of Eastport. At Second Street site the Braun Sausage Works existed (1903-17). A row of attached houses was built at First Street and Jeremy's Way c 1897 for workers at the Severn Glass Company.

During the 1970's many condos were built along the water, and zoning became much stricter. Today not only is Eastport a charming place to live, but has many fine restaurants, boat builders and repairers, yacht sales, sailmakers, sailing outfitters, yacht clubs and marinas.

Places of Interest

The Barge House Museum is one of three shotgun-style structures built in the area. Located at 133 Bay Shore Drive, it is home to the Eastport Historical Committee.

The Seafarers' Club once the Rosenwald School, a segregated "colored" school, is one of eight remaining in Anne Arundel County and was started in 1895. The Eastport Elementary School (now newer building) was started in 1868. The schools were integrated in 1963.

Thompson's and Turner's were two black-owned boatyards.

The McNasby Seafood Company has been around since 1886. It was once one of seven seafood processing plants in Annapolis, closing in 1987, the last oyster shucking place on the Western Shore, but still selling fish.

Chart House Restaurant. Once Annapolis Yacht Yard. Then Trumpy Yachts, maker of famous yachts.

222 Severn Avenue was the site of the Chance Marine (1920-37), Annapolis Yacht Yard, metal shed built for PT boats (1937-47), and Trumpy Yachts (1947-75).

©1998

Naval Academy Chapel

Ginger Doyel

Chapter 9

U.S. Naval Academy

The U.S. Navy was established in 1794, but no formal training had been provided, even though the President was authorized by Congress to appoint 48 midshipmen. A naval school was established aboard the US frigate Guerriere in New York in 1821. Later training was provided on board the US frigate Java in 1882 in Norfolk and in 1833 at the Boston Navy Yard. The very first Naval School (Asylum) began in Philadelphia in 1839 with a one year course. It soon outgrew its space.

The Naval School was established in 1845 by Secretary of the Navy George Bancroft on the grounds of Ft. Severn, then a derelict fort built in 1808 on 10 acres, now the site of present Wing #5 of Bancroft Hall. The fort was deeded over to the Navy from the Army. Ft. Severn had a 14 foot stone wall and enclosed an area 100 feet in diameter. The US War Department had purchased 9 ¾ acres of land from the Dulany family which was called Windmill Point to build Fort Severn. Across the Severn River from the Academy the US government erected Fort Madison, a naval station in 1812.

Congress allocated $28,000 and equipment was mainly "borrowed". Candidates for the school were between 13 and 16 years of age. Ft. Severn, located near the present site of Bancroft Hall, was later roofed over for athletics, and was not razed till 1909. The first Superintendent was Franklin Buchanan. The first June Week dress parade and naval ball were held in 1846, first graduation in 1850 and the first Color Parade in 1871.

The student body, or Brigade of Midshipmen, is made up of approximately 4000 hundred students, instructed by a faculty of over 600. In 1845 the entering class numbered 56 with 7 faculty - 4 officers and 3 civilian professors! These men had a five year curriculum with 2 years spent in Annapolis and 3 years at sea. At that time the first midshipmen wore no uniforms. In 1847 the requirement was changed to a blue cloth jacket, vest and pantaloons.

The Naval School became the United States Naval Academy in 1850, when the four year course was established. During the Civil War the midshipmen were moved aboard the USS Constitution to the Atlantic House Hotel, Newport, Rhode Island. Some of the Southern midshipmen resigned from the Academy, the first W.E. Yancy of Alabama in 1861. In 1862 the Naval Academy was placed under the supervision of the Bureau of Navigation of the Navy

Department. During the War it served as a Union camping ground and military hospital. Rear Admiral David D. Porter became Superintendent in 1865 when the Academy was re-established in Annapolis. About that time the Marine Corps began assigning a detachment to serve as security guards at the Academy.

The official Maryland governor's mansion was located on four acres of Academy land beginning in 1866. 10 acres of land for the Academy was purchased from St. John's College in 1867. 65 additional acres were purchased in 1868, including the cemetery and U.S. Naval hospital. Most of the present buildings were built beginning in 1899 with a $10 million appropriation from Congress. The architect was New Yorker Ernest Flagg, who studied Beaux Arts in Paris. Also in 1899 a U.S. Senate committee rejected a proposal to cut the Naval Academy course from six years to four, and revived " the grade of midshipman...the only proper title for cadets."

During World War I the Academy had about 200 male graduates per year, who completed a three year course. The first ring dance for second class midshipmen was held in 1924. Amelia Earhart was the first female to address the Brigade of midshipmen in 1936. In 1949 the first Black African Wesley A. Brown graduated from the Academy. The first Black student to enter the Academy was James Conyers in 1872. Compulsory reveille and breakfast on Sundays was eliminated by the superintendent, Admiral Smedberg, in 1956. The first female midshipmen started in 1976 with 55 graduating in 1980. Today young men and women complete four years of rigorous training with summers spent at sea, and then serve five years in one of the military services.

Pertinent Information on Visiting the Academy:

The Armel-Leftwich Visitor Center located at 52 King Street (Gate 1) is open 9AM-5 PM March thru December and 9AM-4 PM January thru February. Guided tours leave from here 9:30AM to 3:30 PM Monday-Saturday, 12:15-3:30 PM Sunday (June to Labor Day). Tickets are $5.50, $4.50 seniors and $3.50 students 1st-12th grades. For advance group sales 410-263-6933 ext. 12.

Visiting hours for Academy - 9AM-5PM. Cars and motorcoaches may enter at Gate 1 (end of King George Street), and pedestrians at Gate 1 and Gate 3 (King George Street and Maryland Avenue).

During the Academic year the Brigade holds lunchtime formation in front of Bancroft Hall at 12:10 PM on week days. Formal dress parades are held during the fall and spring on Worden Field. (These depend on weather permitting).

Commissioning Week activities are open to the public except for the day of Commissioning, and special events which need tickets. The Blue Angels give a command performance Commissioning day and rehearsal one day prior.

The Academy also presents athletic programs, concerts, and plays. For information please call the Ticket Office at 800-US-4-NAVY.

The Academy's Worldwide Web home page is http://www.nadn.navy.mil

Buildings and Special Landmarks

The campus known as the Yard (from the English "dockyard") has many buildings of note with the most obvious in sight, and the highest - the Chapel. The Academy has the largest collection of Beaux Arts buildings in the United States.

The Chapel is known as the magnificent "Cathedral of the Navy" and had its cornerstone laid in 1904 by Admiral George Dewey. The architect of the nave, Philippe Cret designed the Pan American Union, the Federal Reserve Building, and the Folger Shakespeare Library in Washington. It is in the shape of a Latin cross and can seat 2500 people.

Tiffany designed many of the magnificent windows. The windows honor several men: "Christ Walking on Water" - Admiral David Dixon Porter, Superintendent 1865-69; the north window (from Gorham) David Glasgow Farragut, the Navy's first four star admiral; "Winged Victory" - Rear Admiral William Thomas Sampson, at the Battle of Santiago. In a smaller window is Sir Galahad representing the ideals of the Navy in memory of Chauncey Bailey Morris Mason. Near the Farragut window "The Invisible Commission" showing an officer's duty to God and to country, the only designed and signed window by Tiffany. Backstar & Gorham designed "Come with Me, I'll Teach You to be Fishers of Men", depicting Jesus, Peter and Andrew. A pew is dedicated to the memory of all POW's and MIA's. The bronze doors were designed by Evelyn Beatrice Longman in 1908 to represent "Father of Invention" and "Mother Country".

The Prayer Book and Bible belonged to David Farragut. Adm. Farragut became a midshipman at age 9 ½, and later first admiral of the US Navy. To the left of the Altar is the Bible of Commodore John Barry who formed the Continental Army in 1775. The organ was installed in 1908 and has been modernized. The Votive Ship hanging in the Chapel is a 12 foot model of a 15th c Flemish carrack, which symbolizes the love of God for sailors. Throughout the Chapel are reminders of the sea - The Naval Hymn "Eternal Father Strong to Save", the windows, scripture, and below the Nave St. Andrew's Chapel, dedicated to the patron saint of the sea. In this chapel is a baptismal font made from wood aboard the USS Constitution. Flanking the front steps are two anchors from the Navy's first armored cruiser, the New York, flagship of Admiral Sampson at the battle of Santiago. The mortars are from the Mexican War.

John Paul Jones, the first Naval war hero is buried in a crypt underneath the high (210 feet) copper dome. His remains were brought here in 1905, 113 years after he was buried in an obscure Paris grave, and his remains found by General Horace Porter, Ambassador to France.

Bancroft Hall- is one of the largest dormitories in the world, covering 33 acres of floor space, 4.8 miles of connecting corridors,and houses all 4,000 students. The Dining Hall, the Ward Room in King Hall, is connected to but not part of Bancroft Hall. The Dining Hall is 65,000 square feet and has 375 tables for 12. The building was designed New York architect Ernest Flagg and built in 1901 in the French Renaissance style.

Naval Academy Museum, Preble Hall - One of the best naval collections in the world with beautiful ship models in the Henry Huddleston Rogers Collection, Navy and Marine Corps history, prints, paintings, flags and many other items.

Tecumsah -"God of the Passing Grade", actually represents Tamenend, chief of the Delaware tribe, is located in front of Bancroft Hall. Prior to all home games, Army Week and for Commissioning he is painted a washable war paint. Before exams pennies are given him for good luck. Tecumsah statue was the figurehead for the USS Delaware, which was scuttled at Norfolk at the beginning of the Civil War.

Herndon Monument - during Commissioning Week the plebes (fourth classmen) climb this monument which has been greased with lard. The first to reach the top must remove the "dixiecup' or plebe cover, and replace it with a combination cover, symbolizing their full membership in the Brigade. Legend has it the first to make it to the top will be the first admiral in the class. Commander William Lewis Herndon lost his Pacific mail steamer and his life, off the coast of Georgia during a hurricane in 1857. His daughter Ellen married Chester A. Arthur, later president of the United States. Maury Hall was named for his brother-in-law, Commander Matthew Maury, a prominent oceanographer.

Ricketts Hall is named for Claude Ricketts, who rose from enlisted man through the ranks to Admiral.

Halsey Field House - named for Adm. William "Bull" Halsey, famous World War II hero. He served as the Commander of the 3rd Fleet Pacific.

Lejeune Physical Education Center. Named for the 1888 graduate, and only Marine Corps general to have command of an Army division.

Dewey Field - was once a boat basin and filled in (54 acres) for athletic fields in 1958. Named for Admiral George Dewey, class of 1858.

Two homes of note on the grounds are the Commandant's House, 8,000 square feet designed by Ernest Flagg in 1904 as a Beaux Arts mansion at 14 Porter Road. The Superintendent's House, also designed by Flagg and known as Buchanan House, 14 Porter Road, was built in 1906 at a cost of $77,539 with 16,000 square feet. It has magnificent gardens and is a grand house for entertaining. Buchanan house is now going through extensive renovations costing $2.5 million. Not only has the house entertained US Presidents, but many visiting dignitaries, receptions for midshipmen and hosts over 15,000 guests a year.

Mahan Hall- named for Adm. Alfred Thayer Mahan, an early graduate of the Academy and naval historian.

Rickover Hall. Built 1975 and named in honor of Admiral Hyman G. Rickover, who urged the use of nuclear power and is known as the "Father of the Nuclear Navy".

Michaelson-Chauvenet Hall was named for two 19th c professors. Mr. Michaelson won the Nobel Prize for Physics by calculating the speed of light. Mr. Chauvenet was the Academy's first mathematics professor, and former head of the Naval Asylum in Philadelphia.

Dahlgreen Hall. Named for Rear Admiral John Dahlgreen, naval ordinance expert during the Civil War and inventor of large calibre naval guns. He commanded the South Atlantic Blockading Squadron during the Civil War. This was originally built as an armory for the Gunnery Department.

Nimitz Library. Named for Fleet Admiral Chester W. Nimitz, a 1905 graduate of the Academy and Commander-in-Chief of the Allied Forces in the Pacific during World War II. 1998 celebrates the 25th anniversary of the library, although the Academy did establish a library in 1845 with 361 books. Professor

William Chauvenet served as the first librarian. The library was moved Mahon Hall in 1907, and the present library dedicated Sept. 7, 1973.

MacDonough Hall is named for Thomas McDonough who won a major b; at Lake Champlain during the War of 1812.

Memorial Hall is dedicated to those graduates who lost their lives serving country. On the balcony is the flag "Don't Give Up the Ship", flown by Olı Hazard Perry at the Battle of Lake Erie September 10, 1813.
The Robert Crown Center, the sailing center, was named for the late Robe Crown, a captain in the US Naval Reserves.

Santee Basin is named after a frigate once anchored at the Academy, which wa; used as a school and prison for the midshipmen.

Mitscher Hall is named for Vice Admiral Marc Andrew Mitscher, Commander-in-Chief of the Atlantic Fleet in 1946. Now the Chaplains' Centre.

Ward Hall is named for Lt. James Harmon Ward USN who was one of the seven faculty members at the founding of the Academy.

Luce Hall is named for Rear Admiral Stephen B. Luce, an authority on seamanship and founder of the Naval War College.

Maury Hall. Lt. Matthew Fontaine Maury was a famous hydrographer.

Alumni Hall is the newest building at the Academy and was built in 1991. Many special events are hosted here, often open to the public.

Worden Field. Rear Admiral John L. Worden USN was the 7th Superintendent of the Academy and Commander of the Monitor during the battle with the Merrimac March 9, 1862. Since 1890 the dress parades have taken place here.

Leahy Hall. Fleet Admiral William Daniel Leahy USN was a former Chief of Staff, Commander-in-Chief of the Army and Navy, and member of the Joint Chiefs of Staff.

Preble Hall. Commodore Edward Preble was commander of the American Fleet during the Tripolitan War. It is the site of the Naval Academy Museum, United States Naval Institute and the Institute Bookstore.

On the harbor side is the foremast of the Maine, sunk in Havana February 15, 1898 and recovered from Havana harbor October 6, 1910.

The Midway Memorial Monument was dedicated in 1996 to those who fought at the Battle of Midway during WWII. Ambassador J. William Middendorf II wrote the "Remembrance Hymn" for the Midway Memorial on Midway when it was dedicated in 1995 for the class of 1942. The monument is in front of Bancroft Hall.

A bronze plate on Chauvenet Walk marks where the house of Judge Joseph Hopper Nicholson stood. He was the brother-in-law of Francis Scott Key from whom he received the original manuscript of "The Star-Spangled Banner" which he set to music. The house was torn down in 1845. Judge Nicholson sat on the Maryland Court of Appeals and served in the US House of Representatives 1799 to 1806.

Farragut Field is named for Admiral David Glasgow Farragut.

Tripoli Monument. Commissioned to honor six naval officers who fell at Tripoli during the Barbary Wars. It was first erected at the Naval Yard in Washington in 1806 as the Naval monument, and damaged when the British burned Washington in 1814. Restoration of the monument was by Benjamin Latrobe. In 1835 it was moved to the west terrace of the US Capitol, and to the Naval Academy in 1860. The monument is the oldest in the Yard.

Mexican War Monument. First monument on Academy grounds, erected to honor four midshipmen who died during the Mexican War.

Macedonian Monument. Originally a figurehead of Alexander the Great on bow of HMS Macedonian of the British Navy, which was captured by Captain Stephen Decatur of the USS United States on October 24, 1812. The figurehead was transferred to the Acadmy from the New York Naval Yard in 1875, and in 1925 became part of the Naval Academy Memorial .

Adm. Ben Moreell Memorial. Honors the founder of the Seabees.

The Naval Cemetery is located across College Creek. The Jeannette Monument honors Lt. George W. DeLong and his crew that died while trying to reach the North Pole across the Bering Strait in1879.

The homes for officers were built along Porter Road, originally called Captain's Row, in 1905 in the French Renaissance style.

Did You Know?

The present Superintendent is Vice Adm. John Ryan, who with his twin brother, Norbert, graduated from the Academy in 1967. Norbert Ryan is a two star admiral who serves as chief of Legislative Affairs at the Pentagon.

The Navy's official song "Anchors Away" was written in 1906 by Charles Zimmerman, the sixth Bandmaster of the Naval Academy for the class of 1907, and son of Charles Z. Zimmerman, a member of the band during the Civil War. Today the Band is led by Ralph Gambone, whose father Ralph also led the band and was part of the group for 25 years! The band was founded in 1853.

The Navy Hymn was written by an Englishman, Rev. William Whiting during a bad storm in the Mediterranean in 1860. He was so glad to have survived the ordeal that he wrote "Travelers by Sea and Land", later known as "For Those in Peril on the Sea". In 1861 this was set to music by John B. Dykes. It was introduced into the Chapel's order of worship in 1879.

The Prayer of a Midshipman was written by Chaplain William N. Thomas in 1938.

The colors of the Academy were changed from red and white to blue and gold in 1892.

"Don't Give up the Ship" was spoken by Captain James Lawrence on board the "Chesapeake" as he lay dying during a sea battle off Boston June 1813. Oliver Hazard Perry took these words to be motto and had his crew hand stitch the flag that from the highest mast of his ship, the Niagara, at the Battle of Lake Erie in September 1813. It is now the slogan for the U.S. Navy.

John Paul Jones was born in 1747 in Kirkkudbright, Scotland and died impoverished in Paris on July 18, 1792. He signed on as a seaman apprentice aboard the merchantman "Friendship" bound for Virginia at the age of 1. He educated himself, not only of the sea, but in other scholarly activities. He worked on a North Carolina plantation in 1775, and then headed to Philadelphia to enlist for the American colonies, and was commissioned a lieutenant. He later commanded the Bonhomme Richard. His major battle was fought in the North Sea against the British frigate "Seraphis", and when asked to strike his colors, he replied "I have not yet begun to fight". He also served as a rear admiral in the Imperial Navy of Her Majesty Catherine of Russia, fighting the Turks in the Black Sea. He returned to Paris ill and poor, and succumbed to his death and was buried in a potter's field. In 1905 his remains were returned to the United States, and in 1913 Congress voted funds for his crypt at the Naval Chapel. The 21 ton sarcophagus of black and white Pyrenees marble was donated by the French government.

Several of the most glorious sailing vessels were once used as training vessels for the midshipmen. They include the "Constitution" (1860-70), "Constellation"- the first commissioned ship in the U.S. Navy and served in every declared war 1799-1955, and "America" (1869-72) later to win the "America's Cup. During the Civil War "America" was purchased by the Confederate army and renamed "Memphis". In 1921 she was sold to the Academy for $1. The first practice sloop was the "Preble" in 1851. The Naval Academy was the co-sponsor of the first Annapolis-Newport Race in 1947. In addition the Academy has participated in Newport-Bermuda races, last winning in 1992.

The Coat of Arms of the Academy is "Ex Scientia, Tridens" "From Knowledge the sea-power". Designed by Park Benjamin an Academy graduate in 1867, and adopted by the Navy in 1898. He also wrote a book entitled "The United States Naval Academy".

A first year student is called a plebe from Latin for "lowest in Roman society". The school year starts in July during which the plebes go through an eight week "Plebe Summer", a strenuous work-out. Midshipman is a British Royal Navy term for an experienced seaman stationed "amidships" between the bow and stern.

The Brigade of midshipmen is divided into two regiments, each with three battalions, and each battalion has six companies. Midshipmen receive one-half the pay of an ensign, the rank they receive on graduation.

All candidates for the Academy must obtain a nomination from an official source. The midshipman graduates with a B.S. degree, and must serve as a Navy or Marine Corps officer.

Dress for midshipmen is "Summer Working Blues", "Summer Whites, "Summer Dress Blues", and "Service Dress Whites".

The mascot of the Academy has been the goat since 1893. The goat is named "Bill" in honor of a former commandant's pet goat. The present "Bill" no. XXVIII dates from 1995. According to legend, a pet goat died aboard a naval vessel in the 1800's. The officers, having fond memories of this animal, decided to save the skin and have it mounted on their return to port. In the meantime they decided to attend a football. Needing an activity during half time, an ensign dressed up in the skin. Needless to say Navy won the game.

The first Army-Navy game was played in 1890. Navy won 20-0. In 1893 the star tackle of the team, Joseph M. Reeves, invented and wore the first football helmet. A forward pass was first used in the Army-Navy Game in 1906. The Academy won the 1926 National Collegiate Football Championship. Roger Staubach and Joe Bellino each won the Heisman Trophy.

The Military Academy at West Point was founded in 1802. Also in that year the first book on naval regulations was published. In it ships' chaplains were instructed to act as schoolmasters for midshipmen.

Admiral Richard Byrd '12, North Pole explorer, captained the 1910 Gymnastics Team.

Franklin Buchanan (1800-64), the first superintendent served as the first admiral in the Confederate Navy during the Civil War.

In 1861 the town of Annapolis was under martial law and the Academy an armed camp. Isaac Mayo who, along with Secretary of the Navy Bancroft had brought the Academy to Annapolis in 1845, resigned his naval position and was dishonorably dismissed by President Lincoln. He had fought in the War of 1812, the Mexican and Indian Wars, and served brilliantly abroad. He is buried in the Naval Academy Cemetery.

The Academy has produced one Nobel Prize winner – Albert Michaelson, a U.S. President - Jimmy Carter, 73 Medal of Honor recipients, 24 Chiefs of Naval Operations, 8 Commandants of the Marine Corps, 4 State Governors and 10 members of Congress, including Sen. John McCain '58, and a former POW. Admiral James Stockdale was also a POW in Vietnam and Vice-Presidential candidate. Admiral Chester Nimitz served as Commander of the Pacific Fleet during World War II. Lt. John Rogers was the first person to fly from the first naval airport at the Academy, flying to the Mall in Washington in 1 hour 20 minutes in 1911 and set the Navy altitude record of 2103 feet. Adm. Schuyler Pyne commanded the New York Naval Shipyard.

Many noted astronauts (47) are also graduates of the Academy - Alan Shepherd '45 (Freedom 7), who was the first American who went into space in 1961 and also landed on the moon; James Lovell '52 (Apollo 13) and Donn Eisele who flew on Apollo 7; Bruce McCandless '58, the first person to walk in space unteethered; Thomas Stafford and Charles F. Bolden (four space shuttle missions), John M. Lounge, Cmdr. Wendy B. Lawrence, William F. Readdy, David C. Leetsma, Capt. Pierre J. Thuot, Bryan D. O'Connor, plus many others. The Freedom 7, America's first space capsule was loaned by the

Smithsonian's National Air and Space Museum to the Armel-Leftwich Visitor Center in 1998.

The American writer, Winston Churchill, a 1894 graduate, wrote the novel "Richard Carvel" while living at the old Carvel Hotel.

Commodore John Barry "Father of the American Navy" was born in Wexford, Ireland, a sister city of Annapolis, and immigrated to Philadelphia. During the Revolutionary War he captained several Colonial Navy ships, and after the war was named the first and senior captain of the new American Navy. The Barry family Bible is on display at the Navy Chapel. Commodore Barry is honored each year with a mass at St. Mary's.

Darwin Robert Merritt, class of 1896 was "the first naval aviator to meet death in the performance of duty".

In 1898 Rear Adm. Don Pascual Cervera and 45 Spanish officers spent several months at the Academy, after his Spanish fleet was destroyed in Havana. These men were taken as prisoners of war, but were received by Captain Edwin White, Commandant of the Academy, and allowed to roam about the Academy and Annapolis at will.

The towers of the High Power Radio Station were erected in 1918 on what is probably the Puritan settlement of 1648. Greenbury Point across the Severn from the Naval Academy is owned by the Naval Academy and the site of these numerous towers that were part of the antenna system owned and operated by the Naval Computer and Telecommunications Area Master Station Atlantic in Norfolk, Virginia. The complex dates back more than eighty years. During World War II all official radio traffic from Washington to the Atlantic fleet passed through the facility. The towers were retired from use in 1995. In mid 1998 the US Senate Appropriations Committee authorized $4.2 million to tear down the towers. Other legislation requires the Navy to create and maintain a permanent wildlife preserve on the 231 acre site.

Until a judgment by the Supreme Court in 1972 midshipmen were required to attend Sunday worship in the Academy Chapel or church of their choice.

In 1874 the US Congress passed an act calling for hazing at the Naval Academy to be investigated by court-martial and punished by dismissal.

1998 marks the centennial anniversary of the Spanish-American War. Many reminders of the war remain at the Academy, including the foremast of the Maine that sank in Havana Harbor. "Remember the Maine" propelled the

United States into war with Spain. The Maine was raised from the harbor in 1912. The mainmast is at Arlington National Cemetery. Adm. George Dewey graduated from the Naval Academy in 1858 and went on to fight in the Civil War and Spanish-American War. Commodore Dewey engaged the Spanish fleet on July 1, 1898 in Manila Harbor, and after the smoke had risen realized he had destroyed the entire Spanish fleet. Two days later Rear Adm. William T. Sampson, a former Superintendent of the Academy and Commodore Winfield Scott Schley were to meet the Spanish Atlantic Fleet off Santiago, Chile. They were to destroy this Spanish fleet.

After the war, Spanish prisoners were brought to a prisoner-of-war camp located on the Academy grounds. Other remnants of the Spanish-American War at the Academy are two guns from the Spanish ship Vizcaya, captured in the Battle of Manila; 6 paintings of the Maine; and anchors from the USS New York, flagship of Rear Adm. Sampson in the Battle of Santiago. These are located in the Naval Academy Museum in Preble Hall. The Reina Mercedes, a Spanish vessel captured at Santiago, was moored at the Academy from 1912 to 1957, and was used as barracks for sailors stationed at the Naval Academy. but was later scrapped.

Football was first played at the Naval Academy in 1879. The first intercollegiate game was played against Johns Hopkins in 1882. Army challenged Navy to the first game in 1890. Two of the better known graduates are Joe Bellino 1961 and Roger Staubach 1965.

For many years the Naval Academy football games were played in Baltimore. By 1948 attendance was declining, due to the new Baltimore Colts team.

In 1923 the Naval Academy announced it would build a 26,000 seat stadium on the site of Farragut Field.

The Marine Corps first sent a detachment to serve as security guards at the Academy about 1865. The men were assigned to quarters in a wharf shed in 1878 with the mess on board a ferry boat. They moved into a new building in 1882, which was later torn down for Dahlgreen Hall. Today the Marines are housed across the Severn River in the North Severn Complex.

The City Dock

Ginger Doyle

Chapter 10

Yachting

Annapolis is the sailing capital of the United States though Newport, San Diego and San Francisco may dispute that title. Pristine and ideally located on the Chesapeake Bay, this town has hosted all manner of boats for thousands of years. The many creeks, rivers and Chesapeake Bay make this a perfect location to start a journey from, keep your boat here or just enjoy the thrill of taking a ride on someone else's.

The Indian dug-out log canoe with a sail was the earliest boat. Later, the settlers used this same style boat. The bugeye is a two-master schooner descended from the canoe, and was used for oystering. The skipjack has a single raked mast and centerboard. Skipjacks dredge by law for oysters under sail on most days and use of a push boat on Mondays and Tuesdays. Only about 30 skipjacks are left. A patent tonger is a vessel that uses rigs and cannot use power for dredging. The season is September 15-March 31.

Included in this section are listings mainly for Annapolis, but other prominent boatyards, boat designers and boat builders.

Famous Yacht Builders

One of the most famous builder and designer of yachts, John Trumpy, purchased the Annapolis Yacht Yard which had constructed the Vosper patrol boats during World War II, and moved from New Jersey to Annapolis in 1947. The site had originally been the Chance Marine Construction Co. founded in 1913 by Charles Chance to build and repair boats for the watermen. During WWI six 110 foot submarine chasers were built for the Navy, and after that boats for pleasure. The Reconstruction Finance Corp. purchased it in 1937, after which it was again purchased, this time by Nelson-Reid, naval architects and boat builders, becoming the Annapolis Yacht Yard, Inc.

The purchase of the yard by the Trumpy's brought in a new era of luxury yachts. During the Korean War John Trumpy and Sons produced 57 foot minesweeping boats and 50 foot "liberty launches. In 1952 John Trumpy retired passing on his duties to his sons, John, Jr. and Donald. At that time the company employed 130 people working on five acres of land in Eastport. Mr. Trumpy remained active in the design of the boats and as Chairman until his death in 1963.

During the Vietnam War Trumpy collaborated on building Nasty-class PTFs (Patrol Boat Fast). By 1971 Trumpy workers were only paid $3.66 an hour and went on a lengthy strike which was to signal the downfall of the yard. The last yacht, the 263rd, Sirius was launched in 1973. The yard's furnishings were sold off, and John, Jr. burned some of the remaining buildings and many of the boat plans. The property was sold. The boat shed is now the Chart House Restaurant. The rest was purchased by Jay Templeton whose estate is presently working on plans to develop the property, which is zoned for "maritime". The book "Trumpy' is a fitting tribute to these master craftsmen.

Another notable boatyard on Spa Creek was founded by Charles Owens who sailed into Annapolis in 1925, having resigned as an executive of Westinghouse Company in Detroit. The Owens Boat Company was one of the earliest dealers for Johnson outboard engines. In 1928 Charles Owens received a US Navy contract to design the very first Knockabouts for the US Naval Academy, which were built by Harvey Mason. Charles Owns, along with his three sons, was later to build cabin cruisers with inboard engines. Mr. Owens died in 1933, but his sons founded the Owens Yacht Company, which was to grow into the second largest recreational boat manufacturer in the US. The company was sold during the 1960's to Brunswick.

Today there are many boats of all sizes built in the Annapolis area. Bruce Farr, a New Zealander has designed many of the boats for the Whitbread races. The wooden boat tradition has been kept alive by Belkov Yachts, the Gardner School, Maynard Lowery on Tilghman Island, and Cutts & Case in Oxford to name a few.

Peter Boudreau has been involved with the restoration of the USS Constitution, a 1845 sloop of war. The USS Constellation is 179 feet long with 20 guns. The ship was used during the Civil War for blockades and patrolled Africa, capturing three slave ships. By 1995 she had deteriorated so badly in Baltimore's Inner Harbor that she had to be removed to a dry-dock next to Ft. McHenry. Volunteers under Mr. Boudreau worked to save her from rot. Mr. Boudreau built the "Pride of Baltimore" II and "Lady Maryland". He served as the captain of the original "Pride of Baltimore". The restoration of the USS Constellation is expected to cost about $9 million, to be raised from private donations.

Ferries, Steamships and Other Vessels

Means of travel to the other side of the Chesapeake was limited until 1952 with the opening of the Bay Bridge to ferries, steamships or other types of vessels. During the 1600's ferries crossed the South River at Londontowne. In the 1760's innkeeper Samuel Middleton operated a ferry across the bay carrying people and horses. The 1830's saw the first steamboats put into operation. In 1919 the 201 foot side-wheeler Governor Emerson C. Harrington began the Annapolis-Claiborne run with cars and passengers in just a little over an hour.

The double-ended Governor Albert C. Ritchie was launched in 1926, an even larger vessel. The John M. Dennis was put into service in 1929 and the terminus was moved from Claiborne to Matapeake, making the crossing in about 45 minutes, and costing 50 cents round trip! The trip from Annapolis was from the King George Street dock. In 1943 this was moved to Sandy Point now taking only 25 minutes. The Dennis made the last crossing in 1952 when the Bay Bridge opened. In June 1973 the second Chesapeake Bay Bridge span opened, one year late and cost $60 million more than the $65 million estimate.

Marine Information

Annapolis Harbormaster. City Dock. 410-263-7973. VHF channel 16
Drawbridge Information. Spa Creek. 410-269-3840. Opens on half hour. Winter by demand
U.S. Coast Guard. 410-267-8107
U.S. Customs (Baltimore). 410-962-8157

Launch Service

Chesapeake Marine Tours, Jiffy Taxi, Naptowne Water Taxi. 410-268-7600. VHF channel 68

Docking and Mooring

The City provides transient docking and moorings services on a first come, first serve basis. Please contact the Harbormaster at 410-263-7973. VHF Channel 16. You cannot anchor within 100 feet of a City mooring, in a marked channel, a no-anchoring area, or where you will hinder navigation. Rafting up is not permitted except with prior approval from the Harbormaster. Landings are free of charge for dinghies under 17 feet. Mooring fees are $15 per day; docking fees vary.

Showers and Rest Rooms

These are available at the Maritime Welcome Center/Harbormasters' Office on City Dock.

Boating Regulations

Speed limit is not to exceed 6 knots.
No wakes
Alcoholic beverages are not allowed on city streets and public property
No swimming or barbecuing is permitted at City Dock
Discharge of waste in water is prohibited
Dogs must be walked on a leash and pooper scoopers used.

Special Yachting Events

Annapolis-Newport Race. Biannually
Wednesday Night Sailing
Frostbiting
Friday Night Beer Can Series
The Whitbread Around the World Race began in Southampton, England September 1997 and one leg came into Baltimore and departed Annapolis April 1998.
Eastport Yacht Club Festival of Lights Parade - held annually in December
Antique and Classic Boat Festival. St. Michael's. 410-745-2916
Leukemia Cup in June.

Yacht Clubs

Annapolis Yacht Club. 2 Compromise Street. 410-263-9279
Eastport Yacht Club- 317 First Street, Eastport. 410-263-0415
Severn River Yacht Club. 519 Chester Avenue. 410-268-8282
Maryland Capital Yacht Club. 16 Chesapeake Landing. 410-269-5219
Severn Sailing Association. 311 Second Street. 410-269-6744

Public Boat Ramps

Sandy Point State Park. 410-974-5975
Truxtun Park. 410-263-7958

Sailing Schools

Annapolis Sailing School. 601 Sixth Street, Eastport. 410-267-7205
Chesapeake Sailing School.7074 Bembe Beach Road. 410-269-1594
J World Annapolis. 213 Eastern Avenue. 410-280-2040
Womanship Inc. 410 Severn Avenue. 410-267-6661

Marinas

Annapolis City Marina. 410 Severn Avenue. 410-268-0660
Annapolis Yacht Basin Company. 2 Compromise Street. 410-263-3544
Mears Marina Annapolis. 519 Chester Street. 410-268-8282
Bert Jabin's Marina. 7310 Edgewood Road. 410-268-9667
Port Annapolis Marina. 7074 Bembe Beach Road. 410-269-1990
Annapolis Landing Marina. Eastport. 410-263-0090
Whitelhall Yacht Yard. 1656 Homewood Landing Road. 410-757-4819
Bluewater Marina. On Rhode River. 410-798-6733

Shipyards/Repairs

Annapolis Boat Service, Inc. 7310 Edgewood Road. 410-280-2935
Annapolis Harbor Boat Yard. 326 First Street. 410-267-9050
Annapolis Landing Marina. 980 Awald Road. 410-263-0090
First Mate Yacht Services. 7416 Edgewood Road. 410-267-7782
J. Hamilton Yachts. 7310 Edgewood Road. 410-263-8785
J. Gordon & Co., Inc. 726 Second Street. 410-263-0054
Muller Marine. 616 Third Street. 410-626-1238
Osmotech-Annapolis, Inc. 722 Second Street. 410-280-9704
Sarles Boat and Engine Shop. 808 Boucher Avenue. 410-263-3661
Whitehall Yacht Yard. 1656 Homewood Landing Road. 410-757-4819
Petrini Yacht Yard and Marina. P. O. 4430. 410-263-4278
Steve's Yacht Repairs. 616 Third Street. 410-268-0092
Yacht Detailing, Inc. 326 First Street. 410-263-4221
Peninsula Yacht Services. Ferry Point Yacht Basin. 410-757-4552
Hartge Yacht Yard. Church Lane. Galesville. 410-867-2188

Cutts & Case Shipyard. Town Creek, Oxford. 410-226-5416
Higgins Boatyard. St. Michael's. 410-745-9303
Yacht Maintenance Inc. 101 Howard Street, Cambridge. 410-228-8878
Oxford Boat Yard. 402 East the Strand, Oxford. 410-226-5101
Crockett Brothers Boatyard. Bank Street, Oxford. 410-226-5113
Andrew Hartge. 519 Chester Avenue. 410-263-6411
Bert Jabins. 7310 Edgewood Avenue. 410-956-2208
Bachelor Point Harbor. Bachelor Harbor Drive, Oxford. 410-226-5592
Campbell's Creek. 109 Myrtle Avenue, Oxford. 410-226-0213
Generation III. 205 Cedar Street. Cambridge. 410-228-2520
Worton Creek Marina. 23145 Buck Neck Road. Chestertown. 410-778-3395
Herrington Harbor North Marina Yacht Yard. Tracy's Landing. 800-297-1930

Towing/Recovery

Ann Bay Towing. 7074 Bembe Beach Road. 410-263-1260
Comprehensive Marine Services. P.O. Box 6308. 410-263-3224
Sea-Tow Services. 1127 Short Street. 410-267-7650
Seaview Marine Service. 410-956-5805

Electric Boat Rentals

Eastport Electric Boat Company. 222 Severn Avenue, Eastport. 410-263-5060

Yacht Dealers/Brokers

Zahniser's Yachting Center. 245 C Street, Solomons. 410-326-2166
Interyacht. 7076 Bembe Beach Road. 410-269-5200
Bristol Yacht Sales. 623 Sixth Street. 410-280-6611
Farr International, Inc. 613 Third Street. 410-268-1001
Wagner-Stevens Yachts. 410-263-0008
Annapolis Yacht Sales. 7416 Edgewood Road. 410-267-8181
Sail Yard Inc. 326 First Street. 410-268-4100
Brittania Boats Ltd. P.O. Box 5033. 410-267-5922
Free State Yachts Inc. 64 Old South River Road, Edgewater. 410-266-9060
Hartge Yacht Sales. 4880 Church Lane, Galesville. 410-867-7240
Lippincott Marine. 3420 Main Street, Grasonville. 410-827-9300

Kayaks

Chesapeake Light Craft Inc. "The Kayak Shop". 1805 George Avenue. 410-267-0137

Inflatable Sales and Rentals

The Air Works. 10 Lincoln Court. 410-268-7332

Rigging

Fawcett Boat Supplies. 110 Compromise Street. 410-267-8681
Chesapeake Rigging. 7310 Edgewood Road. 410-268-0956
Annapolis Yacht Systems, Inc. 7074 Bembe Beach Road. 410- 263-1212
Garth Hichens. 107 Eastern Avenue. 410-280-3711
Kato Marine. 7416 Edgewood Road. 410-269-1218
West River Rigging. 831 Shady Oaks Road, West River. 410-867-7835

Marine Electronics

Annapolis Marine Electronics. 303-B Second Street, Eastport. 410-263-2660
Bay Country Electronics. 4 Dock Street. 410-263-3000
Peter Kennedy Yacht Services. 410-280-2267
Yacht Electronics Systems. 410-268-6977
C. Plath/Weems & Plath. 222 Severn Avenue. 410-263-6700

Marine Engines

Bay Shore Marine Engine. 124 Bayshore Avenue. 410-263-8370
Certified Marine Engine Repair Service, Inc. 326 First Street. 410-263-6718
Chesapeake Marine Engines. 922 Klakring Road. 410-268-268-4055
Marine Engine Sales & Service. 528 Second Street. 410- 268-3072
Vosbury Marine & Recreation, Inc. 300 Fifth Street. 410-268-2522

Boat Builders

Belkov Yacht Carpentry. 311 Third Street. 410-269-1777
Craftworks. 7117 Bembe Beach Road. 410-268-1808

Electra-Ghost Canoes. 7117 Bembe Beach Road. 410-268-1808
Mast & Mallet Boatworks, Inc. P.O. Box 151, Galesville. 410-867-1587
Garth Hichens. 7310 Edgewood Road. 410-280-3711
Farr International. 613 Third Street. 410-268-1001
Cutts & Case. Tilghmann Street, Oxford. 410-226-5416

Boat Building Schools

John Gardner School of Boat Building. 410-267-0418

Marine Hardware, Supplies and Clothing

Fawcett Boat Supplies. 110 Compromise Street. 410-267-8681
Bay Monograms. 905 Bay Ridge Avenue. 410-268-0882
West Marine Products. 111 Hillsmere Drive. 410-268-0129
Ocean Outfitters. P.O. Box 4280. 410-267-0021
Oceana Limited. P.O. Box 6691. 410-269-6022
Snyder's Bootery Inc. 170 Main Street. 410-263-4500

Sailmakers

The Cover Loft. 412 Fourth Street. 410-268-0010
Christopher Ford Yacht Canvas. 7416 Edgewood Road. 410-268-7180
Glenn Housley, Inc. Sailmakers. 1810 Virginia Street. 410-263-4913
North Sails Chesapeake. 317 Chester Avenue. 410-269-5662
Quantum Sail Design Group. 951 Bay Ridge Road. 410-268-1161
UK-Allan Sailmakers. Bert Jabin's Edgewood Boat Yard. 410-263-4913
Hood Sailmakers. 616 Third Street. 410-268-4663

Yacht Interiors

Yacht Canvas. 7416 Edgewood Road. 410-268-7180
The Tailored Yacht. 7310 Edgewood Road. 410-263-4913
Chesapeake Yacht Interiors. 922 Klakring Road. 410-263-8300
Yacht Interiors of Annapolis.326 First Street. 410-263-7144

Systems Analysis

American Boat & Yacht Council. 3069 Solomons Island Road, Edgewater. 410-956-1050

Naval Architects/Surveyors

Thomas Gillmer Naval Architect, Inc. 300 State Street. 410-268-2105
Hartoft Marine Supply Ltd. P.O. Box 3188. 410-263-3609
Howell Marine, Inc. P.O. Box 6542. 410-263-4342
Kaufman Design, Inc. 222 Severn Avenue. 410-263-8900
Fred Hecklinger. 410-268-3018

Charters

AYS Charters & Sailing School. 7416 Edgewood Road. 410-267-8181
Annapolis Bay Charters, Inc. 7310 Edgewood Road. 410-269-1776
Conklin Marine Center. 7040A Bembe Beach Road. 410-263-0706
Chesapeake Marine Tours and Charters. 410-268-7601
Haven Yacht Charter. 20846 Rock Hall Avenue. Rock Hall. 410-639-7140

Special Charter Yachts

Patricia Divine - 70 foot gaff rigged, square topsail schooner
Woodwind - at the Annapolis Marriott Waterfront Hotel. 410-263-7837. Woodwind II joined Woodwind in July 1998. These 74 foot boats can be chartered for two hour trips, all day, and can even accommodate overnight guests or be used in match racing.
Private Pleasure - 60 foot Trumpy boat built 1947
Liberte - The Schooner, Inc. 222 Severn Avenue. 410-263-8234
Imagine. 410-626-8470. 76 foot gaff-rigged schooner for charter. She was the overall winner of the 1997 Great Chesapeake Bay Schooner Race.
America's Cup Yacht Charters - during the fall. For further information 410-267-0418
Fantasy – for private parties. 410-729-2066

Special Boats

Independence – Maryland's official boat. The Independence was built by the Canadian Navy in 1944 as a submarine chaser during World War II. She is 118 feet long and is docked at City Dock.

Marine Financing

Jack Martin & Associates. 111 Forbes Street. 410-263-8000

Lettering

Accent Graphics, Inc. 311 Third Street. 410-268-6411
The Raven Maritime Studio. 130 Severn Avenue. 410-268-8639

Seaplanes

Bay Seaplane Service. 410-745-5595

Local Sailing Publications

Spin Sheet. 410-216-9309
Chesapeake Bay Magazine. 1819 Bay Ridge Avenue. 410-263-2662
Cruising World Magazine. 105 Eastern Avenue. 410-263-2484
Soundings Publication. 326 First Street. 410-263-2386
U.S. Naval Institute. U.S. Naval Academy. 410-224-3378
Cruising World Magazine. 105 Eastern Avenue. 410-263-2484
PassageMaker, The Trawler and Ocean Motorboat Magazine. Horn Point Marina. 888-487-2952

Special Organizations/ Trade Associations

Chesapeake Bay Foundation. 162 Prince George Street. 410-268-8816
Marine Trade Association of Maryland. Port Annapolis Marina. 7074 Bembe Beach Road. 410-269-0741
Chesapeake Region Accessible Boating Organization (CRAB) presents sailing opportunities for persons with or without disabilities. They have "Summer Sail Free" on the fourth Sunday of the month May to September. 410-974-2628

Steward Colonial Shipyard Foundation. Near West River Sailing Club. 410-867-7995. The shipyard was established by Stephen Steward in 1753 to build commercial vessels, and later ships during the American Revolutionary War. It is now home to the Chesapeake 20 fleet.

Well Known Annapolis Sailors Past and Present

John Paul Jones, hero of the American Revolutionary War, is buried in the crypt at the Naval Academy Chapel.

Gary Jobson won his status through America's Cup fame, and is now a CNN telecaster. He was instrumental in getting the Whitbread Around the world Race to the Chesapeake, and is a major supporter of yachting events worldwide.

Bruce Farr is a New Zealander who built two America's Cup boats, including the 1987 "Kiwi" and more recently designed "Chessie Racing", and seven other boats for the Whitbread. He is president of Bruce Farr & Associates. Mr. Farr has designed 16 of the 21 boats in the Admiral's Cup race, mainly Mumm 36's.

Bates McKee, a true gentleman sailor, who is now sorely missed.

Jim Muldoon, owner of the new Donnybrook, once had Starlight Express (also Donnybrook) which set the record for the Annapolis-Newport Race in 1987 with a time of 53 hours and 31 minutes.

George Collins is the owner of Moxie and sponsor of Chessie Racing, the Chesapeake entrant in the 1997-98 Whitbread Around the World Race.

Chris Larson of North Sails-Chesapeake (won 1996 J/24 World Championship and was 1997 Rolex Yachtsman of the Year), Gavin Brady, Geoff Stagg of Farr International, Grant Spanhake, and Terry Hutchinson of Quantum Sail design sailed in Admiral's Cup in England 1997.

Charlie Scott won J24 Worlds and has raced in many other events.

Some Annapolis members of the 1997-98 Whitbread crews included on Chessie Racing were "Fuzz" Spanhake, Dave Scott, Rick Deppe, Jonathan Swain, Greg Gendell, and Gavin Brady.

Walter Cronkite has owned a number of boats named Wyntje, the most recent one a 60 foot Camper Nicholson.

There are many Naval Academy graduates who have contributed to Naval history and sailing. The Academy maintains many lovely boats of all sizes open to the Midshipmen for racing, cruising or day sailing. Graduates include Rear Adm. Robert McNitt author of "Sailing at the Naval Academy"; Nicholas Brown, former director of the National Aquarium in Baltimore; Adm. Holloway, and more recently the twice superintendent Adm. Larson. The Naval Academy is home of the College Sailing Hall of Fame. Adm. McNitt was a recent inductee.

The late Arnie Gay was a former Naval Academy sailing coach and great yachtsman. A marker in his memory is placed at the Eastport end of the Eastport Bridge. For years he ran the C. Gay Yacht Yard on Shipwright Street. He started the Annapolis frostbite series.

Carlton Mitchell, a writer for the National Geographic magazine, won the Bermuda Race 3 times on board "Finnesterre".

Gavin Brady won the 1997 Mumm 36 World Championship on board "Thomas I Punkt".

Tony Smith, owner of Performance Cruising in Mayo, came here in 1973 from England.

Lighthouses

The Chesapeake Bay has many beautiful harbors, but also treacherous shoals. Lighthouses were built to warn the sailors of these, The first lighthouse was built in Maryland in 1822, with 43 added after that. Closest to Annapolis is Thomas Point Lighthouse built in 1875 as a screwpile wooden hexagon, was the last manned lighthouse on the Chesapeake, and was automated until 1989. Sandy Point Shoal was built 1882 as a caisson brick house. Neither of these is open to the public.

Did You Know?

The schooner "America" was used as a training ship for the Naval Academy. In 1851 she won the first America's Cup race "the Hundred Guinea Cup". She was designed by George Steers 95 feet long with 180 ton displacement and carried 5,263 square feet of sail. She was sold in England, and became a Confederate blockade runner. At the end of the war she served as a training ship at the Naval Academy and then was sold to Gen. Benjamin Butler of

Massachusetts. She was given back to the Academy in 1921. During the blizzard of March 29, 1942 she was destroyed at the Annapolis Boatyard when the boathouse roof collapsed.

"Vamarie", a Cox & Stevens wishbone ketch sailed in the 1947 inaugural Newport-Annapolis, now Annapolis-Newport Race, taking 8th in her class. She was destroyed in 1954 by Hurricane Hazel when she was blown against the Naval Academy seawall.

The Penguin, a 12 foot boat, was designed in the 1930's by Phil Rhodes for frostbiting. Bill Heinz of the West River Sailing Club built Hull No. 1. Today they are still seen on the Bay, often as a family boat.

North Sails provided sails for all nine boats in the 1997-98 Whitbread Around the World Race.

The Chesapeake 20 was designed and built by Dick Hartge of Galesville in 1938. A number of these original boats are still around, including at the Chesapeake Bay Maritime Museum in St. Michael's and the Steward Colonial Shipyard Foundation. The Hartge boatyard still produces memorable boats of all sizes and sizes.

Some Important Things to Know about Sailing

Learn how to sail
Take navigation classes
Know the terminology

Know your boats:
Ketch - two-masted, fore and aft rigged boat with mizzenmast stepped forward of rudder.
Sloop - single masted boat with only one headsail
Yawl - two masted fore and aft rigged boat with smaller mizzenmast stepped behind rudder
Catboat - single masted boat with no head sails
Dingy - small racing sailboat

Londontown

Ginger Doyel

Chapter 11

Side Trips on the Western Shore

There are many interesting nearby places to visit. Some of them are very interconnected with Annapolis history and families or ties to nautical traditions. Places included in this section and the one on the Eastern Shore are within a two hour drive from Annapolis. Bay Ridge is part of Annapolis, but like Eastport, maintains its own identity and is a private community.

Bay Ridge

One of the unique communities in Annapolis is Bay Ridge, once a bustling summer resort, and now home to year round residents. This charming area on Tolly Point overlooking the Chesapeake Bay has its own Civic Association, docking and beach facilities on Lake Ogleton.

Bay Ridge was probably sighted by Captain John Smith 350 years ago, at that time inhabited by Indians. A resort was opened in 1880, connected to the region by the Bay Ridge Annapolis Railroad or steamboat. Bay Shore Drive opened in 1887. A long pier extended from the hotel, which also had beaches - 4,000 feet, a bandstand, boardwalk, electric trolley and a restaurant that could seat 1600 guests. Train service stopped in 1899 and Bay Ridge ceased to be a regular steamboat stop. By 1901 the pier had washed away, and in 1903 the resort was closed. To complete its demise the entire structure burned in 1915.

Lots were then sold. The inn (now closed) on the property was built later in 1915. Buildings on the property were used as a rest center for Merchant Marines during World War II. The Soviet Government Purchasing Commission even rented some buildings for a summer retreat for Soviet Embassy personnel, beginning in 1945. Today about 600 homes are spread across the point and nearby. The Bay Ridge Inn which operated until 1997 has now been sold to the Chesapeake Bay Foundation for its headquarters.

London Town

London Town was a tobacco port on the South River beginning in the 17th c, and was considered as a site for the capitol of Maryland. The town was established in 1683 on land given by William Burgess for All Hallow's Parish.

It was the site of the Arundel Court House, built in the mid 1690's and later moved to Annapolis. The community was an agricultural one, and not centered around public buildings or a church. All Hallow's Church in Davidsonville was the local church.

With recent excavations the site was discovered to date back hundreds of years earlier, having been settled by Native Americans of the Woodland Period (AD800-1600). The peninsula was used to harvest oysters, which were preserved by drying in the sun.

Most of the archeological work had centered around the William Brown House completed in 1764, but more recently on London Town. The ravine was known as Scott Street, and at least three more buildings are now known to have existed. Edward and Elinor Rumney operated a tavern as early as the 1690s. Stephen West took over the tavern in 1720. In 1998 a book was published on Dr. Richard Hill, a physician in London Town from 1720-40. He experimented with medicinal plants, some of which are again planted at London Town.

Attractions:
London Town House. London Town Road. 410-222-1919. The house was built for William Brown, a cabinet maker and planter who also ran the ferry across the South River. It has lovely gardens and a rolling lawn down to the South River.

Mayo

Dining:
Old Stein Inn. 1143 Central Avenue. 410-798-6807

Parole

Yes, there is a prison here, but originally this was the site of a Civil War prison - in 1862 a camp for Federal prisoners, which once held 30,000, and over 70,000 passed through. The camp had been moved here from a location on the South River. Prior to D'Epeneuil's Zouaves encamped here. They were a special unit of the Union Army recruited from New York, of many nationalities. In the early 1900's a racetrack was located here.

Attractions:

"Three Mile Oak" - Gen. Washington was greeted here by Generals Horatio Gates and William Smallwood when he came for his resignation in 1783. Rte. 450 and 178.

North of Parole on Rte. 178 is Belvoir, built c 1730 for John Ross, great-grandfather of Francis Scott Key. The grave of Ann Arnold Key, Scott's grandmother is buried on the property. The site during the Revolutionary War was used for a French troop encampment on their way to Virginia.

Crownsville

Crownsville was once home to tobacco and grain plantations. George Washington and his troops passed through here on their way to his resignation of his commission, and Generals Highway is named in his honor. In September and October the Renaissance Fair is held here.

Attractions:
The Rising Sun Inn on Route 17 is owned by the Daughters of the American Revolution, but was used by Gen. Rochambeau during the Revolutionary War as one of his headquarters.
St. Paul's Chapel. Dubois Rd. The chapel was built in 1865 is now the Annapolis Friends Meeting.
Belvoir. Off Wyatts Ridge Road. Francis Scott Key's grandmother is buried in a small plot on what was once the Scott family plantation. The manor dates to 1690. Also in the same plot is Lilibet, a wee child who perished in the manor house fire. The property is privately owned.

The Scottish brown plants (which bloom bright yellow in spring) found along General's Highway are found wild only in this local area. When Gen. Rochembeau arrived during the Revolutionary War with his horses, the food for them was laden with Scottish broom. The horses ate these, the seeds sown, and the plants thrived.

Arnold

Across the Severn River from Annapolis lies the community of Arnold. Indians had settled here, and during the 17th and 18th c tobacco and produce were grown. By 1783 over 500 slaves were known to have lived on Broadneck Peninsula, and following their freedom many stayed on and bought property.

This used to be an area of large farms and summer cottages, but now has a population over 20,000.

The area is named for Thomas H. Arnold, born 1825 who bought land in what is now called Arnold. He was Treasurer of the Annapolis Court House and a farmer. His family donated land for a school, church, cemetery and other buildings, plus managed Arnold's Store.

Dining:
Deep Creek Restaurant and Marina. 1050 Deep Creek Avenue. 410-974-1408

St. Margaret's

This town is named for St. Margaret's, Westminster, London and was founded in 1692. The present St. Margaret's Church built in 1895, was the parish church for all of Broad Neck Peninsula. The property was bought from Dr. Zachary Ridout, a member of the Annapolis Ridout family.

Shady Side

Capt. Salem Avery House. 1418 E.W. Shady Side Road. 410-867-2866. Built 1860 on the West River.

Dining:
Restaurant Peninsule. Cedarhurst Road. 410-867-8664

Davidsonville

All Hallow's Episcopal Church. Rte. 2 and Church Road. All Hallow's Episcopal Church is one of the oldest parishes in Maryland and was registered as early as 1657. The original parish was comprised of about 80 acres bounded by the South, Patuxent and West Rivers. The main crop was tobacco. William Burgess, a planter, provided the establishment in 1683 of the new town for the parish to be located on the South River, which later became London Town.
The official charter was bestowed on May 10, 1692 when William and Mary established the Church of England in the English Colonies with 30 parishes, and it was one of four parishes established in Anne Arundel County. . The Rev. Joseph Colebatch, rector 1698-1734, was designated as the first bishop of Maryland by the bishop of London. However the Maryland courts issued a writ of ne exeat and he was not permitted to go to London to be consecrated. He

occupied Larkins Hundred, built c 1704. The birth of Thomas Chaney was recorded as born on the March 1, 1669. Some of his descendants still live near here. Queen Anne succeeded King William in 1702 and gave the parish its silver communion set.

The present church is a lovely brick built in 1729. From 1784-1792 Mason Locke Weems, the biographer of George Washington was rector.

Just south of Larkins Hundred and Larkins Hill was Etowah Farm, built c 1824, and once owned by Anna Lee Marshall, sister of Robert E. Lee.

Whitehall Farm c1780 located on Route 3 was the birthplace in 1795 of Johns Hopkins, founder of Johns Hopkins University. He was a successful merchant and set aside 47 million for the establishment of the university and hospital.

Middle Plantation on Route 424 near Davidsonville was a 600 acre tract presented in 1664 to Mareen Duvall, esq., a French Hugenot and Commissioner for Advancement of Trade.

Annearrundell Free School. 1290 Lavall Drive. One of the oldest schoolhouses mandated by the colonial government, built 1723. Open Sunday afternoons.

Pasadena

Pasadena was settled in 1890. A silk company bought property here to grow silkworms, but the endeavor failed. The name comes from the owner's wife's hometown of Pasadena, California.

Dining:
Cheshire Crab. 1701 Poplar Ridge Road. 410-360-2220

Severna Park

North of Annapolis is the lovely town of Severna Park. In 1648 Christopher Randall acquired a land grant of 2600 acres, named "Randall's Purchase", that to later become Severna Park. The area is surrounded by the Chesapeake Bay, and the Magothy and Severn Rivers. In 1896 Elizabeth and Tom Boone sold a piece of their land to the Baltimore and Annapolis Short Line railroad which became Boone Station. Many homes grew up around this area.

In the early 1900's Baltimoreans came here as a summer retreat. The town now has a population of over 34,000, many of whom commute to Baltimore or Washington.

Dining:
O'Shea's. Benfield and Jumpers Hole Roads. 410-315-8055
Moulin de Paris. 578 Benfield Road. 410-647-7699
Szechuan Inn. 550 Benfield road. 410-544-0227
Woodfire. 580 P Ritchie Highway. 410-315-8100
Garry's Grill. 553 B&A Blvd. 410-544-0499
Café Bretton. 849 Baltimore-Annapolis Blvd.
Vera's Bakery and Café. 548 Baltimore-Annapolis Blvd. 410-647-3337

Glen Burnie

Restaurants:

Roy's Kwik Corner. 1002 Crain Highway. A winner in the Maryland Seafood Festival for crab soup.

Bowie

The town is named for Governor Oden Bowie. It was first known as Huntington City at the junction of two rail lines, and the station was known as Bowie Station. Much of the town is on the tobacco fields of Belair Plantation patented in 1683.

Attractions:
Belair Mansion. 12207 Tulip Grove Drive. 301-805-5029 was the home of Governor Samuel Ogle, built 1745. Governor Ogle arrived in Maryland in 1731 at the request of Charles Calvert, fifth Lord Baltimore. Gov. Ogle owned a home on Prince George Street in Annapolis, which is now the headquarters of the Naval Academy Alumni Association. The property was bought by Mr. Tasker and Mr. Ogle in 1737 on five hundred acres, which they increased to 2,000 as a working tobacco plantation. Mr. Ogle lived there with his wife, Anne Tasker Ogle, who moved to the Slayton House on Duke of Gloucester Street, Annapolis after his death. Benjamin Ogle, son of Samuel Ogle, was governor of Maryland 1798-1801 owned the house after Col. Benjamin Tasker.

Gov. Ogle was the first to import thoroughbred horses from England, two famous ones being Spark and Queen Mab. His brother-in-law Benjamin Tasker, later owner of the house also owned the mare, Selima. In 1898 the house was sold to William Woodward of New York, president of the Hanover National Bank, whose son was to inherit the house and from whose stable came Gallant Fox and Omaha, two horses who won the Triple Crown. The Woodward Cup Race is named for this family. The stables and house are open to the public. The Woodward portraits of horses hang in the Woodward Wing of the Baltimore Museum of Art. William J. Leavitt purchased the property in 1957. From 1964 to 1978 Belair Mansion was the Bowie City Hall.

Fairview was the home of Gov. Oden Bowie, founding president of the Baltimore and Potomac Railroad.

Huntington Railroad Museum. 8614 Chestnut Avenue. 310-809-3088

Dining:
Mare e Monti. 15554-B Annapolis Road. 301-262-9179. Good Italian fare

Crofton

Crofton was once the site of several large plantations. Some of the land was inhabited by Jesuits who later sold 600 acres called "AynoBrightseat to the Duvall family. Mareen duvall, a French aristocrat, was granted a charter by Lord Baltimore to found a plantation on the South River. This became known as Middle Plantation, and still exists on Davidsonville Road. Later Barton Duvall was to buy other plantations in the Crofton area. His son, Ferdinand Duvall, was a Confederate infantry captain during the Civil War, commanding a company of Maryland secessionists. After the war he lost the land. He is buried on a site off harrow Lane. His son, Robert E. Lee Duvall moved to Portland, Oregon and became a railroad executive. He came back to Maryland in 1900 to claim his family gravesite, and then returned to Portland. There are today Duvall descendants in this area.

Dining:

Sly Horse Tavern. 1678 Village Green. 410-721-4550
Christopher's 1286 Rt. 3 South. 410-451-1602

Odenton

Located northwest of Annapolis is Odenton, home of the Piney Orchard Ice Forum, the training facility for the Washington Capitals. The Piney Orchard Visitor's Center operates a Farmer's Market, March through October each Wednesday afternoon. Named for Governor Oden Bowie. Odenton was the crossing for two railroads - the Baltimore & Potomac and the Washington, Baltimore and Annapolis.

Odenton was the birthplace of Babe Phelps who played for the Brooklyn Dodgers 1935-41 and Chicago Cubs 1933-34.

Fort Meade

Just west of Odenton is Fort Meade/NSA. The Fort Meade Museum, Medal of Honor Library and the National Cryptologic Museum with old cipher machines and other cryptologic materials are open to the public. Ft. Meade was erected 1917 during World War I and is named after the Commander of the Army of the Potomac during the Civil War, Gen. George Meade.

Linthicum

Benson-Hammond House. Andover Road and Aviation Boulevard. 410-768-9518

Lothian

Lothian is a Scottish name, as are several of the roads such as Greenock. Brooks Woods Road received its name from the Brooks family. Lothian was settled in the early 1700's.

Gambrills

From 1869-1885 Gambills was known as Sappington. It was then named for Dr. Steven Gambrill whose house was at Gambrills and Maple Road. The Naval Academy Dairy Farm is located here. The Hammond Manor House dates c1700 and was owned by the Hammond family until 1913 when it was sold to the Navy. The original owner was thought to be Philip Hammond of Annapolis. Plans are to close this facility in 1998.

Elkridge

The Great Falls of the Patapsco River lie on the northwest side of Elkridge. Elkridge landing was once a port where ships brought goods from England,

and tobacco was shipped out. It was the largest colonial seaport north of Annapolis. Even Captain John Smith knew of the river, and wrote of the red clay.

The first curved stone arch bridge, the Thomas Viaduct, built in America in 1835 spanned the Patapsco River near Elkridge. During the Civil War Union soldiers were stationed to guard the Viaduct as the plantation owners sided with the Confederacy and the mill workers with the North.

Dining:
Elkridge Furnace Inn. 5745 Furnace Avenue

Ellicott City

Ellicot City was once known as Ellicott's Mills. Three Quaker brother, John, Andrew and Joseph Ellicott came to this area in 1771 from Bucks County, Pennsylvania. They grew wheat and power for grinding came from the Patapsco Road. It was the Ellicott brothers who persuaded Charles Carroll, signer of the Declaration of the Declaration of Independence, to plant wheat at his estate Doughoeregan. The Ellicott brothers built roads, a bridge and wharf in Baltimore, introduced the wagon brake, erected iron works, built schools and may other buildings.

Andrew Ellicott and Benjamin Banneker, a free Black man and neighbor, were commissioned to survey the boundaries for the new capital, Washington, DC in 1791. Mr. Banneker later was to build the first clock made in America and to publish Almanacs.

The city was granted a city charter in 1867 and the name changed to Ellicott City. The Baltimore and Ohio Railroad's first 13 miles connected Baltimore to Ellicott City beginning in 1831. The first railroad terminal in the US was built here in 1832.

Attractions in Ellicott City:

Ellicott City B & O Railroad Station Museum. Maryland Avenue and Main Street
Howard County Historical Society.8328 Court Avenue
Montpelier Mansion. 9401 Montpelier Drive
Laurel Museum. 817 Main Street
Stillridge Herb Farm

Patapsco Female Institute. Built on land donated by Ellicott brothers in 1837.
3691 Sarah's Lane
Patapsco Valley State Park
Thomas Isaacs Log Cabin. Main Street and Ellicott Mills Drive
Heritage Orientation Center. Old Court Records Building

White Hall. Chatham Road. Early 19th c home as part of a land grant involving "Freeborn's Progress" and "Dorsey's Search". The main house was built between 1810 and 1820. The acerage passed from Judge Richard Ridgely to Col. Charles Worthington Dorsey, a planter and participant in the War of 1812. Mary Tolley Dorsey was born at White Hall in 1825. She married Thomas Watkins Ligon, the 33rd governor of Maryland. They lived at White Hall upon his retirement. The house was almost destroyed by fire in 1893, and remained unoccupied until Mr. Ligon's son, Charles Worthington Dorsey Ligon, purchased 430 acres and the house in 1900. Mr. Ligon married Harriet Ridout of Annapolis. The house was reconstructed. The house was passed to their daughter, Harriet Govane Ligon Hains and their son-in-law Hamilton Hains. They remained in the house until their deaths in 1988 and 1990. In 1997 the house was sold to William and Annamarie Hugel. It is the Historic Ellicott City's 1998 Annual Decorator Showhouse.

Laurel

Laurel was originally a mill town located on the Patuxent River, and called "Laurel Factory" for all the mountain laurel that grew in the area. The Baltimore and Ohio Railroad began service in 1835 with Laurel a major station.

Attractions:
Montpelier Mansion and Arts Center. Muirkirk Road. The house was built for Major Thomas Snowden in 1774. It is a beautiful Georgian home, and resembles some of Annapolis' lovely mansions such as the Hammond Harwood or William Paca Houses.
Laurel Museum. 817 Main Street. Mill worker's house dating from c 1840

Dining:
Café de Paris. 14252 Baltimore Avenue (Rte. 1). 301-490-8111
Pasta Plus Restaurant & Market. 209 Gorham Avenue. 301-498-5100. Good Italian food

Savage Mill

Savage Mill was established in 1822 by Amos Williams and his three brothers with $20,000 borrowed from John Savage. The mill wove mainly canvas for sails used by clipper ships. And from the Civil War through World War II the canvas was used for tents, cots, bags, cannon and truck covers. The Bollman Truss Bridge was brought to Savage Mill in 1860 and was an early bridge for the B & O railroad line.

Attractions:
Bollman Truss Bridge
Historic Savage Mill. Built 1821-22 and used until 1947. Now has very nice shops and restaurants.

Annapolis Junction

This town is not adjacent to Annapolis, but 3 ½ miles northeast of Laurel. A line of the B&O Railroad passed through here to Annapolis. It was once called Centralia as it was midway between Washington, Annapolis and Baltimore.

Baltimore

Baltimore has its own guidebooks and history, but there are several special places to be visited. 1997 marked the 200th anniversary of Baltimore and many celebrations were planned. Baltimore's history is very linked to Annapolis as Baltimore took over as the prominent Maryland port from Annapolis in the late 18th c. Also horse racing came to this area with Gov. Ogle and today flourishes to the north and south of the city.

Some key attractions are very much related to Annapolis history:

Homewood Museum. 3400 N. Charles Street. 410-516-5589 This Federal mansion was built by Charles Carroll, Jr. in 1801 and includes Carroll family furnishings.

Carroll Mansion (Baltimore City Life Museums). 800 East Lombard Street. 410-396-3523. This home was built by Charles Carroll of Carrollton, the last surviving signer of the Declaration of Independence, who wintered in the Federal-era mansion from 1820 until his death in 1832. His granddaughter, Mary Caton, was considered one of the most beautiful women in Baltimore. She married Robert Patterson whose sister at the time was married to Jerome, brother of Napoleon Bonaparte. Their grandson Charles J. Bonaparte served as US Secretary of the Navy and Attorney General in Theodore Roosevelt's cabinet. After Mr. Patterson's death she moved to England and married the Marquess Wellesley, the Duke of Wellington's brother.

Baltimore Maritime Museum. Inner Harbor. 410-396-3452. The museum has three historic ships, including the lightship "Chesapeake" and the Coast Guard cutter Taney, named for Roger Brooke Taney, Chief Justice of the United States, whose statue is at the State House in Annapolis. The Taney was the only warship still afloat that saw action December 7, 1941 at Pearl Harbor.

Fort McHenry National Monument. E. Fort Avenue. 410-962-4290. In September 1814, Francis Scott Key, a graduate of St. John's College, Annapolis, wrote the "Star Spangled Banner". At the time he was a lawyer. The original manuscript is owned by the Baltimore Historical Society.

"The Flag House". 844 East Pratt Street. Home of Mary Pickersgill who made the 30 X 42 foot flag that flew over Ft. McHenry on September 13, 1814 when Francis Scott Key wrote the "Star Spangled Banner".

Today Baltimore has a new Roman Catholic Cathedral, but the first one was planned by Bishop John Carroll, the first Roman Catholic Bishop of the United States and a cousin of the Annapolis Carrolls. The Cathedral was designed by Benjamin Latrobe. Bishop Carroll was invested as an Archbishop here in 1808. The funeral mass of Charles Carroll of Carrollton was held here in 1832.

"Pride of Baltimore II". Replica of 1812 Baltimore sailing clipper. Inner Harbor

The National Aquarium. 501 Pratt Street. 410-576-3800. The former Director was Nicholas Brown, a graduate of the Naval Academy.

Maryland Historical Society. Monument Street. Original manuscript of "The Star Spangled Banner".

Peale Museum. Holliday Street. Built by Rembrandt Peale in memory of his father Charles Willson Peale

Mount Clare Museum House. Built beginning in 1756 and finished 1760 for Charles Carroll the Barrister, author of the Maryland Declaration of Independence and member of the Continental Congress. He had studied in England and most of the materials used in building the house were sent from there. He also maintained a home in Annapolis, now demolished but said to resemble the Jonas Greene House, and married Margaret Tilghman, his cousin. Charles Carroll in 1766 contributed to a purse to enable Charles Willson Peale, a saddle maker in Annapolis, to study painting in England. Mr. Peale was to paint oils of the home in 1775, and later portraits of Mr. and Mrs. Carroll, that are presently in the Mount Clare collection.

The house was dramatically changed to a grand Palladium home in 1766-67, influenced by the Upton Scott and Ridout homes in Annapolis. When Annapolis was laid out in 1683-84, it was divided into 100 one-acre lots. At the time of the Barrister's death he owned seven of these.

On July 4, 1828 Charles Carroll of Carrollton, aged 90, laid the cornerstone of the Baltimore and Ohio Railroad at Mount Clare. In 1829 at Mount Clare the New York inventor, Peter Cooper, began to build his experimental locomotive, the Tom Thumb. The house is presently maintained by the National Society of Colonial Dames in Maryland.

Shot Tower. Front at Lafayette Street. The cornerstone for this was laid by Charles Carroll of Carrollton in 1828.

Baltimore Museum of Art. This has some fine examples of John Shaw's furniture.

The Carrollton Viaduct over Gwynns Falls was built in 1829 and was the first stone masonry bridge in the United States. Named for Charles Carroll of Carrollton.

Ladew Gardens. 3535 Jarrettsville Pike. Monkton. 410-557-9570. Harvey S. Ladew developed some of the most spectacular topiary gardens in America between 1929 and 1971. He enjoyed fox hunting and horses and these even appear as topiary. Not only are the gardens lovely, but during the year concerts, lectures and "My Lady's Manor Steeplechase Races" benefit the gardens.

Washington

In 1791 the state of Maryland gave Congress the land to build the District of Columbia. A couple of special places related to Naval history and Annapolis are important to visit.

Washington National Cathedral. Mount St. Alban's. Has the beautiful "Space Window" with a piece of the moon rock, a memorial cross to those who died in the Spanish-American War. Charles Carroll Glover, a banker and civic leader,

131

held a meeting in his Washington home in 1891 to make plans for a national cathedral. Two years later a charter was granted to the Protestant Episcopal Foundation. The Cathedral was part of Major L'Enfant's original plans for the capital.

Bishop Thomas John Clagett and his wife Mary Gantt were buried at Croom, and have since been moved to the Cathedral. Francis Scott Key wrote the inscriptions on their tombstones. Francis Scott Key was a founder of Christ Church, Georgetown and Trinity Church, Washington.

<u>Navy Monument</u>   Pennsylvania Avenue
<u>Navy Base</u>. 8th and M Streets, SE

<u>Dumbarton House</u>. 2715 Q Street, NW. Dolley Madison fled to the home of Charles Carroll when the President's House (the White House) was burned during the War of 1812.

Most of <u>Capitol Hill</u> and southwest Washington was purchased by Thomas Notley, a colonial governor of Maryland (1679-84) in 1691 for 40,000 pounds of tobacco. His godson Notley Rozier inherited the land, and had a daughter Ann who married Daniel Carroll of Annapolis. Her two sons Charles Carroll and Notley Young later inherited the estate part of which was to become the U.S. Capitol and the Navy Yard.

<u>Benjamin Banneker</u>, whose museum is in Annapolis, along with Andrew Ellicott was asked to survey the new capital city in 1791 which was to become Washington

<u>Benjamin Ogle Tayloe House</u>. The house is on Madison Place overlooking Lafayette Square, and is part of the U.S. Court of appeals for the Federal Circuit. Mr. Tayloe was a descendant of several Annapolis families. He is the author of "Our Neighbors on Lafayette Square", published in 1872 and containing many stories about the occupants of the White House, whom he knew.

Galesville

Just a few miles south of Annapolis on the West River is the charming town of Galesville. Settled in 1649 by Quakers it was then called West River Landing. It was an "Official Port of Entry" beginning in 1684. The only military action in Anne Arundel County during the War of 1812 took place on Chalk Point across from Galesville when a party from a British ship went up the West River to the property of Stephen Steward.

In 1832 a German emigre, Henry Hartge purchased 647 acres on the West River with many walnut trees to provide wood for his piano manufacturing business. His grandson, Emile Alexander Hartge was to purchase 17 acres on the other side of the river 1879 at White Stake Point. The Hartge Yacht Yard is on that site. They became renowned boatbuilders of the Chesapeake 20s. The name was changed to Galesville in 1924 in honor of Richard Gale, a Quaker planter. Woodfield's Fish and Ice Company is now run by the fourth generation of Woodfield's.

Today the town is filled with antique shops and boutiques. Good seafood restaurants entice many people to travel down from Annapolis. Among them are the Inn at Mary's, Pirate's Cove for lunch, the Topside Inn and New Steamboat Landing.

Attractions:
Tulip Hill. On West River near Galesville. Land patented to Richard Talbot in 1659. Built 1755-62 for Samuel Galloway, a wealthy merchant and Quaker. Named for tulip poplar trees, some believed to be over 400 years old. Samuel Galloway owned Selim, a famous horse of the 18th c.

Cedar Park. On tract of land bought by Richard Galloway in 1697. John Francis Mercer, Governor of Maryland 1801-03, later lived in the house.

Portland Manor. MD Rte 408. Once on 1,000 acres granted to Col. Henry Darnell by Lord Baltimore in 1697. Col. Darnell was " Receiving General, Chief Agent and Keeper of our great seal at Arms in our Province".

On Rte. 255 is the West River Quaker Burial Ground. The West River Meeting was founded c 1671. The first general meeting of the Friends was held here. Many Quakers lived in this area, but later joined the Protestant Episcopal Church.

Highland Beach

The town was founded in 1893 by Charles R. Douglass, son of abolitionist Frederick Douglass as a summer retreat for Blacks.

Solomons Island

Solomons was once known as Somerville Island. It lies one mile from the mouth of the Patuxent River on the north shore. Capt. Isaac Solomon established an oyster business here in 1867, and the area once had a large oyster fleet. Deep water oyster tongs and bugeyes came from here. The J.C. Lore Oyster Processing Plant operated from 1888 to 1978. The causeway is built on a bed of oyster shells. The P. .uxent enters the Bay, and though only a few watermen still work out of here, Solomons has become a very popular boating haven, and many homes have sprung up with Washington only sixty miles away and Annapolis a bit closer. During World War II (1942-45) troops were trained for amphibious landings adjacent to the Calvert Marina.

Attractions:
Calvert Marine Museum. 410-326-2042. The J.C. Lore house is now part of this museum. There is much history of the area here, and particularly its relationship with watermen, and fossils from Calvert Cliffs. Drum Point Lighthouse was was first commissioned in 1883 to guard the entrance to the Patuxent River, and is a screwpile lighthouse. It was moved and restored to Solomons in 1975. The Wm. B. Tennison is the oldest Coast Guard-licensed passenger carrying vessel on the Chesapeake. The nine-log chunk-built bugeye was built in 1899. It was converted from sail to power and served as an oyster buyboat until 1978.
Cove Point Lighthouse
Chesapeake Beach Railway Museum. Rte. 261

Lodging:
Davis House. Charles and Maltby Stree's. 410-326-4811
Holiday Inn and Conference Center. 155 Holiday Road. 410-326-6311
Myrtle Point Bed and Breakfast. Over Thomas Johnson Bridge. 301-862-3090. C1860
Bowens Inn. 14630 Solomon's Island Road South. 410-326-9814
Grey Fox Inn. 410-326-6826
Adina's Guest House. 14236 South Solomons Island Road. 410-326-4895
Back Creek Inn. Calvert and Alexander Streets. 410-326-2022
By-the-Bay. 14374 Calvert Street. 410-326-3428
Solomons Victorian Inn. 125 Charles Street. 410-326-4811. On harbor
Webster House. 14364 Sedgwick Avenue. 410-326-0454

Restaurants:
Lighthouse Inn. Solomons Island Road. 410-326-2444
Solomons Crabhouse. Rte. 2/4. 410-326-2800
Solomons Pier. Solomons Island Road. 410-326-2424

CD Café. 14350 Solomons Island Road. 410-326-3877

St. John's Creek

Annemarie Garden on St. John's Creek. Located three miles north of Solomons Island is a magnificent garden donated by Francis and Ann Koenig to Calvert County in 1993.

Sotterly Plantation

This was once part of a 4,000 acre grant given to Thomas Cornwallis by Lord Baltimore in 1650 and called Resurrection Manor. It was subdivided in 1710 with 890 acres, and was purchased by James Bowles. He began construction on the main house but died in 1727. His widow married George Plater II, a lawyer, who with his son George Plater III (sixth governor of Maryland) completed the house. His widow was later to marry Edward Lloyd of Wye House (see Eastern Shore).

George Plater V lost the home in a game of chance in 1822 to Col. Sommerville. Col. Sommerville sold the estate to Thomas Barber and his step-daughter Emeline Dallam, who married Dr. Walter Briscoe. The plantation was bought by Herbert Satterlee, a New York lawyer, in 1910. Sotterley was the name of the Satterlee family home in Suffolk, England c 1066. It has a lovely view to the Patuxent River and an English garden. (OTP)

St. Mary's County

The county was founded in 1637 and named for the Virgin Mary as the colonists landed here on the Feast of the Assumption 1634.

St. Mary's City

The original Catholic capital of Maryland was founded in 1634 by Leonard Calvert who arrived on board the "Dove" and "Ark" with 128 people, including Mathias de Sousa, the first Black to arrive in Maryland. It served as a tobacco plantation and capital until 1695 which was moved to Annapolis, and St. Mary's almost died out.

One of the more famous people from St. Mary's was Margaret Brent (c 1601-1671) who grew up in Gloucestershire, England, and in 1619 converted to Roman Catholicism. Her father lost most of his estate, due to his non-Anglican stance, and Margaret and three of her siblings decided to move to the Maryland colony with thousands of acres through land grants. Margaret and her sister Mary lived on 70 acres in St. Mary's, called "Sisters Freehold". Margaret became very involved in community affairs, and was eventually asked to act as the sole executor of Leonard Calvert's estate. Lord Calvert was governor of Maryland, and the younger brother of Lord Baltimore. She has been titled "America's first litigator". The American Bar Association's Commission on Women in the Profession has named The Women Lawyers of Achievement Award for her.

Attractions:
St. Mary's College is rated one of the "best small schools in the U.S."
The "Dove" - replica of the original boat the settlers arrived on Maryland shores.
Governor's Field - town green
1676 State House - reconstructed Statehouse
Father White Memorial erected to honor Jesuit priest who traveled with the first settlers on board the "Ark" and "Dove:.
Trinity Church. Bricks came from original Courthouse 1676
Godiah Spray Tobacco Plantation.
Margaret Brent Memorial Garden
Farthing's Ordinary
Cross Manor. Patented to Thomas Cornwaleys, one of Leonard Calvert's commissioners 1638, and later deputy governor

St. Michael's Manor

St. Michael's Manor is located near Point Lookout. 301-872-4025. It was one of three manors granted to Leonard Calvert in 1639. Present house built by James I. Richardson c 1805. Now B&B

Preston on Patuxent

This town was the capital of Maryland 1654-1659. The land was patented to Richard Preston in 1652 and purchased in 1676 by Capt. Richard Ladd who left it to Christ's Church. It was later bought by the Johnson family (Governor Thomas Johnson was first Governor of Maryland, and his niece married President John Quincy Adams).

Port Republic

Attractions:
American Chestnut Land Trust. Scientists Cliffs Road. Hiking. Arboretum
One-Room Schoolroom. Broomes Island Road. Over 100 years old.
Christ Episcopal Church. 3100 Broomes Island Road. Started as log church
1672. Present brick church dates from 1762.

Lusby

Attractions:
Calvert Cliffs Nuclear Power Plant. 1650 Calvert Cliffs Parkway. 410-495-
4673. 19th c tobacco barn has exhibits on archeological and agricultural
products from area, and on nuclear power. First nuclear power plant in
Maryland.
Calvert Cliffs State Park. Rte. 765. Almost 1500 acres. Trails. Cliff formed
over 15 million years ago. Fossils
Middleham Episcopal Church. Rte. 765. Established 1684

Chesapeake Beach

Attractions:
Chesapeake Beach Railway Museum. Mears and C Streets. 410-257-3892. A
railway once ran from Washington and Baltimore to the beach, built by Otto
Mears, a Colorado railroad builder. He wanted a "Monte Carlo on the Bay", but
most often it was frequented by working class people from Washington. The
railroad folded during the Depression, and the town was to suffer from gas
rationing during World War II and the closing of the amusement park.
However, it still attracts people who have now basically retired here and
winterized the cottages and new homes were built. The railway station is the
museum.

St. Edmonds United Methodist Church. 3000 Dalyrmple Road. Built of logs in
1865 with assistance from Freedman's Bureau. Served freed blacks as church
and school. Church burned in 1882 and church rebuilt 1928.

Newtown Neck

The town was patented 1640. In 1677 Father White, the Jesuit priest who
traveled with the settlers on the Ark and Dove founded the antecedent of

Georgetown University. St. Francis Xavier Church dates from 1640, the present structure 1731.

Chancellor Point

The point is 2 miles SW of St. Mary's City on the St. Mary's River. It is named for Philip Calvert, brother of the Second Lord Baltimore, who was chancellor of this province.

Point Lookout

This area is located below St. Mary's and was named St. Michael's Point by Leonard Calvert. In 1862 it became a Civil War hospital, then a prison, Fort Lincoln, for captured Confederates after the Battle of Gettysburg holding 52,264 prisoners of whom 3,364 died. The poet Sidney Lanier was one of those held here. Now Point Lookout State Park.

St. Clement's Island

The original settlers brought over by the second Lord Baltimore landed March 25, 1634 on St. Clement's Island in the Potomac, and celebrated the first Roman Catholic Mass here.

Attractions:
St. Clement's Island-Potomac River Museum. Colton's Point. 301-769-2222

Port Tobacco

Port Tobacco was built where the Potomac River meets the Port Tobacco River. Capt. John Smith sailed up the Potomac in 1608 and marked the Indian village of Potopaco, which was colonized by the English in 1634. A Jesuit missionary Father Andrew White converted the Indians and translated the catechism and other English works into the Indian language in 1638. The Jesuits had been given four thousand acres in this region. Father White was later tried in England for being a Catholic priest. He was acquitted, but never returned to Maryland.

Saint Thomas Manor on Chapel Point is home to the beautiful church of St. Ignatius with its historic cemetery, built in 1798. The cornerstone of the church was laid by Bishop John Carroll, first Bishop of the United States. The Manor House next door was built in 1741. It had quarters for slaves given to the Jesuit priests. Slavery ended here in 1839. Pastor Francis Neale brought the Carmelite nuns to the US and settled them in this parish.

A 1727 Act of the Maryland Assembly planned for the building of a courthouse and village in the vicinity, and named the town "Charles Town". However Port Tobacco got its name from the thousands of pounds of tobacco annually shipped from here, and was the second largest river port, behind St. Mary's City until the Revolutionary War.

The first religious community for women was founded at the Mount Carmel Monastery in 1790. In 1808 the courthouse and Episcopal church were blown down in a windstorm. The courthouse was rebuilt, but burned in 1892. With the silting of the river the county seat was moved to La Plata in 1895.

The courthouse was restored with state funds starting in 1965. Other places of note are the Chimney House (1765), Stag Hall (1732), The Charles County Museum of Port Tobacco, and the Birch House c 1700. The Society for the Restoration of Port Tobacco continues its work to preserve this charming place of the past

Among the famous people who lived here were Thomas Stone, a Signer of the Declaration of Independence at "Habre de Venture" (built 1771-73) - now Thomas Stone National Historic Site; John Hanson, first elected President in Congress Assembled at "Mulberry Grove"; Major-General William Smallwood (Revolutionary War) at "Smallwood's Retreat"; Daniel of St. Thomas Jenifer, signer of the U.S. Constitution at "Retreat"; Dr. Gustavus Brown, the Washington family physician at "Rose Hill"; and Dr. James Craik, Surgeon General of the Continental Army at "La Grange".

St. Leonard

Joshua Barney was one of the heroes of the War of 1812. He also lobbied the Maryland legislature in Annapolis to build a fleet of boats to harass the British in the Chesapeake, but the legislature refused. He instead got that money from the US Congress. On St. Leonard's Creek in 1814 during a naval battle, Joshua Barney's barges were cornered by the British. They were burned rather than allowed to fall into British hands. Recent discoveries by archeologists have found what they believe are the remains of a gunboat used by Capt. Barney.

Attractions:
Jefferson Patterson Park & Museum. 10515 Mackall Road. 410-586-8500. 544 acre park on Patuxent River. Trails, archeology, special events.

Lexington Park

Attractions:
Naval Air Test and Evaluation Museum. Rte.235. U.S.' only museum dedicated to testing and evaluation of naval aviation. Models, photographs. The Test Pilots' School is where astronauts Glenn, Shepard, Schirra and Carpenter trained. Alan Shepard served two tours at the Patuxent River Naval Air Station. He arrived in 1950 to attend the US Naval Test Pilot School, and later in the 1950's to test aircraft and teach at the school. He was one of the original seven Mercury astronauts, the first to go into space and one of only 12 men to walk on the moon. Alan Shepard was a graduate of the Naval Academy, and died July 1998.

Glenn Dale

Marietta. 5626 Bell Station Road. 301-464-5291. This is a lovely plantation once owned by the Duvall family. Gabriel Duvall built the home in 1811, the year he was appointed an Associate Justice on the Supreme Court. He was also a member of the Maryland House of Delegates, the U.S. Congress, the Maryland State Supreme Court, and Comptroller of the U.S. Treasury. The house remained in the Duvall family until 1902 and is now open to the public.

Upper Marlborough

Attractions:
Darnell's Chance. 14800 Governor Oden Bowie Drive. 301-952-8010. This home was constructed between 1694 and 1713 and is the probable birthplace of Daniel Carroll, a signer of the US Constitution and his brother John Carroll, the first bishop of the Roman Catholic Church in the US.
W.H. Duvall Tool Museum. Patuxent River Park. 16000 Croom Airport Road. 301-627-6074
Merkle Wildlife Sanctuary and Visitor Center. 11704 Fenno Road. 301-888-1410
Old Maryland Farm. 301 Watkins Park Drive. 301-249-6202
Patuxent River Park. 16000 Croom Airport Drive. 301-627-6074
Billingsley Manor. 301-627-0730

Clinton

Surratt House and Tavern. Brandywine Road. 301-868-1121. The house was built in 1852 for John and Mary Surratt. During the Civil War it was a safehouse for the Confederate underground. In 1864 John Wilkes Booth left some of his possessions here. On fleeing from Washington after President Lincoln's assassination, he stopped here for them. Mary Surratt was tried as a co-conspirator and on July 7, 1865 became the first woman to be executed by the federal government. The building is now a museum.

Havre de Grace

The author could not complete this book without mentioning Havre de Grace. Although, she was born in Baltimore, she spent her first few months in Havre de Grace, with her maternal grandparents nearby. The town is the northernmost on the Chesapeake, across from Chesapeake City, it has a fascinating history, and one of the most photographed lighthouses on the Bay, Concord Point Lighthouse. The British burned almost 60% of the houses during the War of 1812.

Attractions:
Concord Point Lighthouse. Foot of Lafayette Street. Built 1827 by John Dunahoo
Decoy Museum. Giles Street
Thomas Hopkins House. 229 N. Union Avenue. Built 1839 for Dr. Thomas Hopkins, a member of the Maryland legislature 1842-43 and 1865-66.

© 1998

Ginger Doyel

Chesapeake Bay Skipjack

Chapter 12

Eastern Shore

Maryland's Eastern Shore is connected to the state by the Bay Bridge, but indeed one steps into a different world here. There are an abundance of creeks, peninsulas, islands, wildlife, oystering and crabbing, watermen, and tobacco plantations and people proud of their love of the water where a slower lifestyle abounds. Nestled along the creeks and rivers, or even in backyard sheds are energetic and enthusiastic boat builders and designers, and boatyards that produce everything from classic yachts to watermen's boats.

Days can be spent wandering among these places, taking in some antiqueing and sightseeing along the way. Ferries and bridges, many of them drawbridges, cross some of the rivers and creeks. You truly do not know what will appear around the next corner. The "Traveling Brushes", a group of Eastern Shore ladies may be painting away on an obscure creek, or cruising aboard a skipjack. Geese may fly over, heading north or south.

Some of the author's favorite towns are here highlighted. Make sure you acquire a good map of the Eastern Shore as it is very easy to get lost, or on a road where the only way out is the way you came in.

Kent Island

Kent Island is just across the Chesapeake Bay Bridge from Annapolis and is separated from the Eastern Shore by the Kent Narrows. It is the largest island in the Chesapeake. The first court opened in 1639. The area was claimed before Lord Baltimore in 1631 by William Claiborne of Virginia, who built a trading port. The first settlement was established on the south side of the island. Claiborne built a church, fort, farms - including starting Maryland's tobacco economy, and other buildings, though none of this exists today. He brought the first white woman to Maryland, Joane Young. Lord Baltimore also claimed the island and the first naval battle in the colonies took place here.

Christ Church was founded at the fort and was moved to Broad Creek in 1652. A ferry operated from Broad Creek to Annapolis. Nearby were the first courthouse and jail on the Eastern Shore. Broad Creek became a town in 1683. Later Stevensville, Dominion and Chester took over as ports. Tobacco, wheat and corn were the major crops.

Steamers and the railroad were later to come through Kent Island, bringing many visitors, many of whom stayed at the Love Point Hotel. The hotel had Saturday night dances, an amusement park and boardwalk.

Before the opening of the Bay Bridge a ferry ran from Matapeake. Kent Narrows is noted for seafood processing and has about 12 establishments.

Attractions:

Christ Church. 117 East Main Street. Stevensville. Congregation founded 1631. Present church c 1880.

Cray House. Cockey's Lane. Stevensville. Mansard roof cottage built 1815.

Stevensville Train Depot. Cockey's Lane. Dates c 1902

Stevensville was named for Stevens Adventure the tract of land on which it was built.

Broad Creek was founded in 1686 and was a stop on the postal route established by the Maryland Assembly in 1695. Later it hosted a terminus for the two ferries from Annapolis.

Wildlife Trust of North America at Horsehead Wetlands Center. 600 Discovery Lane. Grasonville. There are over 300 acres of beautiful marshland here. One can walk trails, visit the waterfowl research facility, or attend special events.

Restaurants/Hotels

Kentmorr Restaurant. Kentmorr Road, Stevensville. 410-643-2263. Waterfront dining.

Kent Manor Inn. 500 Kent Manor Drive, Stevensville. 410-643-5757

Harris' Crab House. Kent Narrows, Grassonville. 410-827-9500

Chester River Inn. Tackle Circle Road. 410-643-3886. Built c 1857-60 by Tolson family on land once owned by William Body and called Body's Neck in 1650.

Lands End Manor on the Bay. 232 Prospect Bay Drive. Grasonville. 410-827-6284

Hemingway's. 410-643-CRAB

Café Sophie. Stevensonville

Verna's Island Inn. 800 Main Street. Stevensonville

Anglers Restaurant & Marina. Grasonville. 410-827-6717

Island Inn. 800 Main Street. Stevensville. 410-643-2466

Fisherman's Inn. Kent Narrows. Grasonville. 410-827-8807

The Narrows. 3023 Kent Narrows Way S. Grasonville. 410-827-8113

Arnie's Steak and Seafood House. Mears Point Marina. 410-827-7103

Fisherman's Crab Deck. Kent Narrows. 410-827-6666

The Jetty Restaurant. Rte. 50, Exit 42, Kent Narrows. 410-827-8225

Pelican Bay. Queen Anne Marina. 410-643-0230

Queenstown

Queenstown was the first county seat of Queen Anne's County, and a port during War of 1812. In 1813 the British attacked Queenstown with 1400 men in two groups. They were forced to return to their ships when one group was routed by 18 men and the other group landed in the wrong place and were cut off from town by Queenstown Creek.

Attractions:
Colonial Courthouse. Rte. 18 and Del Rhodes Avenue. C 1708

Lodging:
The House of Burgess Bed and Breakfast. 7109 Main Street. 410-827-3396. House built c 1840s.
Irish Bed and Breakfast. 511 Pintail Point Road. 410-827-7029

Centreville

The settlement of St. Paul's Parish dates back to 1692. The town was incorporated in 1794. Centreville replaced Queenstown as the county seat of Queen Anne's County in 1782.

Attractions:
The County Courthouse is the oldest in continuous use in Maryland. 100 Courthouse Square. Built in 1792. In front is a statue of Queen Anne dedicated by HRH Princess Anne.
Tucker House. Commerce Street. Built 1792. Lovely herb garden
Wright's Chance. 125 Dulin Clark Road. 410-758-0166. C 1744, but on original tract dating from 1681. Contains items owned by William Paca. Now headquarters of Queen Anne's Museum of Eastern Shore life
St. Paul's Episcopal Church. The Communion silver dates to 1717, church from c 1699, when it cost 14,395 pounds of tobacco to build.
Chesterfield. Chesterfield Avenue. Estate of William Helmsley granted 1660
Gunston Hall School. 410-758-0620. Preparatory school, founded in 1911
Fairlee Manor, near Centreville, was owned by actress Tallulah Banhead who donated it to the Easter Seals Society for a summer camp.
Queen Anne's Museum of Eastern Shore Life. 126 Dulin Clark Road.

Lodging/Restaurants:
Rose Tree B&B. 116 S. Commerce Street. 410-758-3991. Built 1794
Lighthouse Pub. 511 Chesterfield Avenue

Kennedyville

Shrewsbury Episcopal Church. Route 213. Parish established 1692. Church c 1835.

Church Hill

Church Hill once had six churches in town.

Attractions:
St. Luke's Episcopal Church. Rte. 19. Is the oldest brick church in Maryland, dating back to 1732. The church cost 140,000 pounds of tobacco.
Eastern Shore Tea Company. 800-542-6064. This unique company blends teas, including "Chestertown" to commemorate the Chestertown "Tea Party" and the "Peggy Stewart" of Annapolis "Tea Party" in 1774.

Sudlersville

Sudlersville dates from the mid 18th c and was named after the Sudler family who settled at "Sledmore". Famous baseball player Jimmy Foxx was born and raised here.

Attractions:
Train Station Museum. 101 Linden Street. Dates c 1885
Dudley's Chapel. Benton Corner Road. This is the oldest Methodist church in Queen Anne's County dating to c 1783 and fifth oldest in the U.S.

Hunting Lodge:
J&P Hunting Lodge. 1105 Benton Corner Road. 410-438-3832

Chestertown

Chestertown was once called New Town and is located on the Chester River. The first courthouse was built in 1697, and the town laid out in 1706 on one hundred acres divided into equal lots. On April 19, 1706 the Act for Advancement of Trade and Erecting Ports and Towns in the Province of Maryland was signed into law. Cambridge received its present name in 1780. Washington College was founded here in 1782. Money was made from wheat, corn and hogs, and later Port of Entry for tobacco and the Eastern Shore. The artist Charles Wilson Peale was born here. It is the seat of Kent County.

Chestertown was a port during the Revolutionary War. In 1774 a protest near the Customs House was held against the Tea Tax. The William Geddes brigantine was boarded and the cargo thrown overboard. This event is still reenacted on May 24 and 25th.

The Kent County News is "A Direct Descendant of the Chestertown Spy" established in 1793 and one of the oldest newspapers in the United States.

Chestertown is one of the most beautiful towns along the Chesapeake Bay with charming homes built along the river and side streets and rolling lawns down to the river. There are many antique shops and delightful restaurants. Once here you may never want to leave. The best time to explore is during the week, when there are not hoards of people.

Attractions:
Geddes-Piper House. 101 Church Alley. 410-778-3499. Built eariy 1700's home of William Geddes, customs collector for the Port of Chestertown. Later sold to James Piper, a merchant. Now site of Kent County Historical Society.
Customs House. High Street. c 1730
Washington College. Built 1783-88. The 10th oldest institution of higher learning in the US is the only college to receive George Washington's consent to use his name. He did visit the college in 1784 and contributed $233.33 to the Endowment Fund.
Nicholson House. Queen Street. Built 1788 for Capt. John Nicholson who served in the Continental Navy in command of "Hornet" and with his brother Samuel of the "Deane" during Revolutionary War.
Widehall. 101 Water Street. Built c 1770 for Thomas Smythe, Kent County's wealthiest merchant. Later owned by Robert Wright, governor of Maryland 1806-09 and Ezekial Chambers, U.S. Senator 1820's and Maryland judge. Widehall has beautiful gardens.
River House. 107 N. Water Street. Built by Richard Smythe of Widehall 1784-87. This was once the home of the first president of the Board of Visitors and Governors of Washington College. Now owned by the Maryland Historic Trust.
William Barroll House. Built 1735
Frisby House. 110 Water Street. Built 1770
Emmanuel Protestant Episcopal Church. Cross Street. Erected 1768. Noted Tiffany window. The rector Dr. William Smith presided over the convention that changed the name from Anglican Church of the United States to Protestant Episcopal Church. He also founded Washington College and was elected Maryland's first Episcopal bishop in 1784, a bid later withdrawn.
Hynson-Ringgold House. Cannon and Front Streets. The house was built on land owned by Nathaniel Hynson in 1735 It was later purchased by Thomas

Ringgold 1767, a wealthy merchant. William Buckland designed the antler staircase. Since 1944 this has been home for presidents of Washington College. Schooner Sultana Project. 346 Cannon Street. 410-778-6461. The Schooner Sultana Project is an undertaking of the Chester River Craft and Art, a nonprofit organization, to build and operate a reproduction of the schooner "Sultana". The boat was an American built boat, purchased by the British Royal Navy in 1768. It monitored colonial shipping preceding the Revolutionary War.

Kent County Court House. Court Street. Constructed 1860 at a cost of $11,254.

Richauds Branch-Langford Road, just outside Chestertown, was one of the first turnpikes in the U.S. Tench Tilghman, Secretary and Aide to General Washington, rode this route from Virginia to Philadelphia to inform the Continental Congress of General Cornwallis' surrender during the Revolutionary War. St. Paul's Episcopal Church is along this road. It was founded in 1693, though the present building dates from 1713. It was used as a barracks during the War of 1812. The actress Tallulah Bankhead is buried here. Also on this road is Remington Farms, a wildlife preserve open to the public.

B&B and Hotels:
The Imperial Hotel. 208 High Street. 410-778-5000. Lovely Victorian Hotel that also serves delicious meals.
The Inn at Mitchell House. Rte. 21. 410-778-6500. 18th c
The White Swan Tavern. 231 High Street. 410-778-2300. Built 1733, became tavern in 1793. The tavern was operated by Joseph Nicholson, whose two sons were famous naval officers during the Revolutionary War. Serves afternoon tea.
Great Oak Manor. 10568 Cliff Road. 410-778-5943. Lovely Georgian home on property that once numbered 1100 acres, but now only 12 acres.
The Parker House. Spring Avenue. 410-778-9041
Brampton B&B. 25227 Chestertown Road. 410-778-1860. Greek revival built 1860
Widow's Walk. High Street. 410-778-6864
Radcliffe Cross - B&B. Built 1725
Lauretum Inn B&B. Rte. 20. 1-800-742-3236. Once owned by U.S. Senator George Vickers (1801-79)
Stillwater Inn Bed and Breakfast. 7109 Second Street. 410-827-9362
Claddaugh Farm B&B. 410-778-4894
The Rolph Inn Bed and Breakfast at Rolph's Wharf. 1008 Rolph's Wharf Road. 410-778-6347

Restaurants:
Andy's Pub. High Street. 410-778-6779
Old Wharf Inn. Cannon Street. 410-778-3566. Great location on the river.

Ironstone Café. Cannon Street
Feast of Reason. High Street. 410-778-3828. Deli
Sharon's Diner. 323 High Street. 410-778-2940
Blue Heron Café. Cannon Street. 410-778-0188
The Café. 410-810-4929
The Channel Restaurant. 21085 Tolchester Beach Road. 410-778-1400
Caulk's Field. Rte. 20 and Rte. 21. 410-810-0932
Black Eyed Susan's. 601 Washington Avenue. 410-778-1214

Tolchester

Tolchester is located near Chestertown. It was built as a fancy resort in 1877 complete with hotel, racetrack and steamers to carry people to other parts of the Chesapeake. The only battle during the War of 1812 took place here in 1814. The British officer Sir Peter Parker landed forces, and he was killed. The battle was known as Caulk's Battle.

Rock Hall

This town was once known as Rock Hall Crossroads, and was established 1707. The ferry used to sail from here to the western shore. Tench Tilghman began his ride from Rock Hall to announce the surrender of the British at Yorktown to the Continental Congress in Philadelphia.

Attractions:
Watermen's Museum. Next to Haven Harbour Marina. 410-778-6697. Models of Chesapeake boats- bugeyes, log canoe, pungy, dory, and other watermen relics.
Waterman's statue. Route 20
Eastern Neck National Wildlife Refuge
Eastern Neck Island was one of the first places to be settled on Chesapeake. Wickcliffe house built 1650's. Wickes Memorial honors Capt. Lambert Wickes, Revolutionary War hero who lived in house.
Caulk's Field- important battle between British and Maryland militia fought here 1814.
Trumpington. About five miles from Rock Hall. Land grant dates from 1658. In 1687 Thomas Smythe purchased the property for 6,000 pounds of tobacco. His daughter Sarah married Matthew Tilghman, speaker of the House of Delegates 1791. The house still remains in the Smythe family.

Restaurants:
Watermans' Crab House. Sharp Street Wharf. 410-639-2261
Swan Point Inn. Rock Hall Avenue at Coleman Road. 410-639-2500
Durdings Store. 5742 Main Street. Old fashioned drugstore with soda fountain
America's Cup Café. 410-639-7361 Bookstore and coffee shop
Bay Wolf. 410-639-2000. Austrian cuisine
Old Oars Inn. Main Street. 410-639-2541
Osprey Point Restaurant. Swan Creek. 410-639-2762
Ford's Seafood, Inc. Rte. 20. 410-639-2727
Tolchester Marina's Channel Restaurant. 21085 Tolchester Beach Road. 410-778-0751

Lodging:
Moonlight Bay. Lawton Avenue. 410-639-2660
Bay Breeze Inn. 5758 Main Street. 410-639-2061
The Inn at Osprey. 20786 Rock Hall Avenue. 410-639-2194
Huntingfield Manor. 410-639-7779

Betterton

Betterton, like Tolchester, was also a resort town, and is located on "Fish Hall Farm". Steamboats brought guests to this town developed by Richard Turner. The town is named for his wife, Elizabeth Betterton. The town still has a beach and attracts those wishing to relax along the Chesapeake Bay.

Georgetown

Georgetown is located on the Sassafras River, and was a Port-of-Entry, a ferry landing, and a base for Continental supplies during the Revolutionary War. The British burned the town in May 1813

Lodging and Dining:
Kitty Knight House. Route 213. 800-404-8712. Only house in Georgetown and Fredericktown not burned by British during War of 1812 when the owner refused to leave an invalid neighbor.
Carrousel Horse Inn. 145 Main Street. 410-648-5476
The Granary. MD Route 213, on Sassafras River. 410-275-1603. A favorite of the author's since she was a little girl.

Galena

Galena was formerly called Downs Cross Roads, and renamed for the silver found here in 1813 and carried to Philadelphia. The mine was closed down during the War of 1812 so the British wouldn't use it.

Rosehill Farm is 4th largest miniature rose nursery in the U.S.

Lodging:
Rose Hill B&B. 13842 Gregg Neck Road. 410-648-5334

Millington

Millington was built on a tract of land called "London Bridge', owned by Daniel Massey 1794. The town was founded by Thomas Gilpin, a Quaker. It was originally called "Bridgetown" and later "Head-of-Chester". It received its present name from Richard Millington, a farmer.

Attractions:
Old Mill. Sassafras Street. The mill was built in 1766.

Wye Island

Much of Wye Island consists of a 2,800 acre registered wildlife preserve.

Attractions:
The Old Wye Church dates c1721 and is one of the oldest Episcopal churches in the United States.

Wye Plantation was once owned by Governor William Paca as a summer home. The present mansion was built in 1972 for Arthur Houghton, President of Steuben Glass. The grounds have trees over two hundred years old, boxwood gardens, and is truly one of the grand Eastern Shore estates.

Wye House has been in Lloyd family since 1658. The present house was built c 1784 and has lovely gardens. The place was named after the Wye River in Wales, from where the Lloyd's had emigrated.

Wye Oak State Park

Wye Oak State Park is off Route 50. Wye Oak. The oak is the official tree of the state of Maryland. The largest white oak and one of the oldest in the United States is located here.

The Wye Mill is a grist mill dating from c1682. In 1706 Richard Sweatman operated a saw mill and two grist mills here. It produced cornmeal for Gen. Washington's Continental Army. There is only one grist mill operating today.

Easton

Part of Easton was Cooke's Hope, a land grant given to Major Miles Cooke by the Lord Baron of Baltimore in 1695. Easton was originally called Talbot Court House, later Easton and county seat for Talbot County beginning in 1788. It was incorporated in 1790. Much of town was destroyed in fires 1810, 1855 and 1878. Easton Point had a fort to protect Easton during the War of 1812.

In November the Waterfowl Festival, the premier of its kind, attracts people from around the world (410-822-4567).

For something really special, take a ride in a vintage biplane at the Easton Airport. Call 410-820-5959.

Attractions:
The Third Haven Friends Meeting House. 405 S. Washington Street. The house was built in 1682, and is the oldest religious building in the U.S. William Penn preached here with Lord Baltimore present.
The Historical Society of Talbot County. 25 South Washington Street. 410-822-0773. The Society maintains the James Neall House b 1810 and Joseph Neall House b 1795.
Bullit House. Built 1790
Foxley Hall C 1795
Hughlett Henry House. Built c 1795
Academy of Arts. 106 South Street, famous American artists represented.
Christ Church. 111 South Harrison Street. The church was founded in 1692, and is the fifth place of worship for St. Peter's Parish. The present building was built 1840-45 of Port Deposit granite.
Talbot County Courthouse. 11 North Washington Street. The first courthouse was built in 1712. The present one dates from 1794. The "Talbot Resolves" were adopted here, and later incorporated into the Declaration of Independence.

On July 31, 1783 five Masonic Lodges met here to form the first Grand Lodge of Masons in Maryland.

Talbot Free Library. James Michener's proofs and other memorabilia were given to the library after he spent much time using the Maryland Room for his research for "Chesapeake"

Thomas Perrin Smith House. .Washington Street. Built in 1803. Now Chesapeake Bay Yacht Club.

Avalon Theater. 40 E. Dover Street. 410-822-0345. The building was constructed in 1921. The theater has presented outstanding shows and performers, and was the scene of three world premiers included "The First Kiss", starring Fay Wray and Gary Cooper in 1928.

White Marsh Church. Now in ruins, contains grave of Robert Morris, died 1750.

Tuckahoe State Park. Arboretum, hiking, picnicking.

Pickering Creek Environmental Center. 400 acre preserve.

Lodging:
Tidewater Inn and Conference Center. 11 East Dover Street. 410-822-1300
Ashby 1663. 27448 Ashby Drive. 410-822-4235
John S. McDaniel House. 14 N. Aurora Street. 410-822-3704. Built 1890. Each floor has a turret.
Bishop's House. 214 Goldsborough Street. 410-820-7290. Built for Philip Francis Thomas, governor of Maryland 1848-51. In 1892 sold to Episcopal Church and was the residence of the Bishop of the Diocese of Easton.
Chaffinch House B&B. 132 S. Harrison Street. 800-861-5074
Gross' Coate Plantation 1658. 11300 Gross' Coate Road. 410-819-0802

Restaurants:
Crystal Café. 201 Marlboro Avenue. 410-822-2224
The Kitchen. 22A N. Harrison Street. 410-819-6780
Washington Street Pub. 20 N. Washington Street. 410-822-9011
Café 25. 25 Goldborough Street. 410-822-9360
Tom's Tavern. N. West Street. 410-770-3710. Steakhouse
Yesteryear's. Easton Plaza. 410-822-2433
House of Hunan. 201 A Marlboro Road. 410-820-4015
HG. Rt. 50. 410-822-1085
Restaurant Columbia. 28 S. Washington Street. 410-770-5172
Rustic Inn of Easton. Talbottown on Harrison Street. 410-820-8212
Legal Spirits. 42 E. Dover Street. 410-820-0033
Mason's Café. 22 South Harrison Street. 410-822-3204
Fiddle Leaf Café. 12 W. Dover Street. 410-822-4353
Railway Market. 108 Marlboro Street. 410-822-4852

Oxford

The town was founded in 1683 and used as a Port of Entry in 1694, along with Anne Arundel (Annapolis). It was incorporated 1706 and eventually became a haven for Quakers and Acadians who emigrated from Canada. Oxford was once Maryland's largest port.

The Oxford-Bellevue ferry has been operating since 1683, either as a scow propelled by sail, or by other means. Today the ferry is the oldest, non-cable ferry in the United States. It is just an easy hop over to St. Michael's, unless you want to drive around. The cost is $5 for the 10-15 minute ride.

Lt. Col. Tench Tilghman, an important Revolutionary War hero is buried here. He was General Washington's aide-de-camp and personal secretary and carried news of the British surrender at Yorktown to the Continental Congress. Col. Tilghman was one of the first people to use the Hussey reaper developed by Obed Hussey of Union Town, Maryland. Plimhimmon, the Tilghman family home dates from a land grant in 1659.

The replica of the customhouse stands next to the Tred Avon Yacht Club in The Strand and was originally located on the other side of the Tred Avon. After the Revolution Oxford lost its importance as a port, and tobacco was no longer shipped from here. The railroad arrived in 1871 stimulating growth of the seafood processing business. By the 1880's steamboats brought visitors who stayed along The Strand.

Today Oxford remains a boat building and watermen center. There are few oyster boats left, but oystering and crabbing are still important. Oxford is a delightful town, has many lovely old buildings, and during the summer is a favorite stop for yachtsmen.

Attractions:
Academy House. 205 N. Morris Street. Was officers' residence for Maryland Military Academy 1845-55.
Barnaby House. 212 N. Morris Street. Built 1770's by Capt. Richard Barnaby, a sea captain.
Byberry & Calico. On grounds of Cutts & Case. Byberry is oldest house c 1695.
Oxford-Bellevue Ferry. N. Morris Street and The Strand. Believed to be oldest privately operated ferry in U.S. operating since 1683. The first keeper was Richard Royston.
Oxford Museum. Morris and Market Streets
Tench Tilghman Monument. Oxford Cemetery on Rte. 333.

Customs House. N. Morris Street. Replica of 18th c customs house used by Jeremiah Banning, the first federal collector of customs

Grapevine House. 309 N. Morris Street. The grapevine in the front was brought from the Isle of Jersey in 1810 by Captain William Willis, who commanded the brig "Sarah and Louisa".

Lodging:
Robert Morris House Inn. 314 N. Morris Street. 410-226-5111. Home of Robert Morris, signer of the Declaration of Independence. Built 1710. He was known as the "Financier of the American Revolution".

The 1876 House. 110 N. Morris Street. Oxford. 410-226-5496. Built 1876

Oxford Inn and Pope's Tavern. 504 S. Morris Street. 410-226-5220. Built by F.A. Delahaney Overery as an inn at turn of the century.

Combsberry. 4837 Evergreen Street. 410-226-5353. Built 1730. Elegant English country home on Brigham's Cove.

1876 B&B. 110 N. Morris Street. 410-226-5496

Nichols House. 217 S. Morris Street. 410-226-5799

Restaurants:
Jacqueline's. 202 S. Morris Street. 410-226-0238

Le Zinc. 101 Mill Street. 410-226-5776

Pier Street Marina and Restaurant. 410-226-5171

Pope's Tavern. 504 S. Morris Street.410-226-5005

Robert Morris Inn. 314 N. Morris Street. 410-226-5111

Schooner's Llanding. Foot of Tilghman Street. 410-226-0160

Bringman's. Morris Street. Confectionery

Royal Oak

Lodging:
The Pasadena Inn. Rte. 329. 410-745-5053. B&B

A Part of Retreat B&B. 26004 Rte. 329. 410-745-3980

St. Michael's

St. Michaels was settled in 1677 and incorporated in 1804. The town was named for St. Michael the Archangel. The river was named Myles in 1675 by William Hambleton of Martingham. The area was noted for shipbuilding, and it has many historic homes, shops and a beautiful harbor.

In 1770 an Englishman, James Braddock, purchased land and laid it out in lots. In 1805 a central area was set aside for the public market house, St. Mary's Square. On the square is the ship's carpenter's bell cast in 1841 that rang at 7AM, noon and 5PM to measure the workday for the ships' carpenters who worked in the nearby shipyards.

The author James Michener lived on Church Neck overlooking Broad Creek from 1977 to 1983 while he researched and wrote "Chesapeake". He never returned and his house was sold in 1996. Some of his neighbors included Sen. George McGovern and Graham Kerr, the "Galloping Gourmet".

Historic Sights:

Cannonball House – Mulberry Street and St. Mary's Square. Only home damaged by British War of 1812. C 1805. Built by shipwright William Marchant.

Tarr House. Built c 1661 by Edward Elliott as his plantation. Mr. Elliott and his indentured servant, Darby Coghorn built the first church in St. Michael's about 1677, on the site of the present Episcopal Church (6 Willow Street).

St. Mary's Square. Laid out in 1770 by James Braddock. Lovely homes and St. Mary's Square Museum. 19th c home of "half timber" structure. The site was originally patented to John Hollingsworth in 1659.

Chesapeake Bay Maritime Museum- Mill Street. 410-822-3456. Boats, models, decoys. Once site of crab picking and processing plants. The Hooper Strait Lighthouse, built in 1879 and the Knapp's Narrows Bridge have been moved to the museum grounds. The bridge is a bascule bridge, weighing 108 tons. The Museum bought it from the state for $1.

The Footbridge. The bridge joins Navy Point to Cherry Street. The bridge has had several names, including "Sweetheart Bridge" and "Lover's Bridge".

Bruff House. On land sold to John Bruff in 1791 for 20 pounds and remained in his family until the mid 1900's.

Amelia Welby House. Built 1700's from brick and now covered in mahogany siding. This was once the home of the first "Poet Laureate of Maryland"

"The Cottage". Original home of shipwright Robert Lambdin and his descendants 1840 to 1905.

"The Old Inn". Talbot Street at Mulberry. Built c 1816 by Wrightson Jones, who owned and operated the shipyard at Beverly on Broad Creek.

Mill House. Harrison Square. The house was originally built on the beach c 1660, and later moved.

Christ Episcopal Church. 301 S. Talbot Street. The church was erected in 1878 of Port Deposit stone.

Perry Hall. This was once owned by Comm. Perry and was the site of the 1998 Eastern Shore Designer Showhouse. It is now owned by the Marine Engineer's Beneficial Association (MEBA) and sits on 350 acres.

Inns and B&Bs:

Inn at Perry Cabin. 308 Watkins Lane. 410-745-2200. Elegant inn on water owned by Laura Ashley family. The original house was built in the 19th c by Samuel Hambleton, a purser in the United States Navy during the War of 1812. The house was named for his friend, Commodore Oliver Hazzard Perry.

Parsonage Inn. 210 N. Talbot Street. 410-745-5519. Built 1883 by Henry Clay Dodson, a prominent St. Michael's businessman and legislator. Mr. Dodson and Joseph White founded the St. Michael's Brick Company.

Harbourtown. Rte. 33 at Martingham Drive. 410-745-9066 (resort)

Victoriana Inn. 205 Cherry Street. 410-745-3368. The house was built in 1873 by Dr. Clay Dodson, a U.S. army officer during the Civil War.

Wades Point Inn on the Bay. 410-745-2500. Named for Zachary Wade who received a land grant in 1657. Thomas Kemp, the original builder of the "Pride of Baltimore", built the 1819 farmhouse.

Kemp House Inn. 412 Talbot Street. 410-745-2243. Georgian built 1807 for shipwright and soldier Col. Joseph Kemp

Beacon Hall. 103 N. Harbor Drive. 410-745-9494

Brick House B&B. 202 N. Talbot Street. 410-745-2799

Cove Guest House. 9241 Deepwater Drive. 410-745-5142

Dr. Dodson House B&B. 200 Cherry Street. 410-745-3691

Fleet's Inn. 200 E. Chew Avenue. 410-745-9678

The Getaway B&B. Long Haul Creek. 410-745-2094

Hambleton Inn. 202 Cherry Street. 410-745-3350. The waterfront house was built in 1860.

Little House on Chestnut Street. 120 W. Chestnut Street. 410-745-9347

Rigby Valliant Hous B&B. 123 W. Chestnut Street. 410-745-3977

Snuggery Guest House. 203 Cherry Street. 410-745-3558

Tarr House B&B. 109 Green Street. 410-745-2175. One of St. Michael's oldest houses

Two Swan Inn. Carpenter Street. 410-745-2929. The house was built in the 1800's and served as the former site of the Miles River Yacht Club.

Victoriana Inn. 205 Cherry Street. 410-745-3368

Escape Hatch. 310 S. Talbot Street. 410-745-6360

Mt. Misery B&B. 23946 Mount Misery Road. 410-745-6811

The Old Brick Inn. 401 S. Talbot Street. 410-743-3323

Restaurants:

Crab Claw Restaurant. Navy Point. 410-745-2900

208 Talbot. 208 N. Talbot Street. 410-745-3838

Inn at Perry Cabin. 410-745-2200. The inn serves some of the finest food in the U.S. and afternoon tea.

St. Michael's Crab House. 305 Mulberry Street. 410-745-3737

Town Dock Restaurant. 125 Mulberry Street. 410-745-5577. During the War of 1812 this was known as Dawson's Wharf. In the 1950's "The Longfellow Inn" was on this site. It burned, and the present building was constructed in 1977.
Justine's. Talbot and Cherry Streets. Old fashioned ice cream parlor
Bistro St. Michael's. 403 S. Talbot Street, 410-745-9111
The Buttermilk Café. 306 N. Talbot Street. 410-745-2224
Morsels. 205 N. Talbot Street. 410-745-2911
Poppi's Restaurant. 207 N. Talbot Street. 410-745-3158
Suddenly Last Summer. 106 N. Talbot Street. 410-745-5882
Yesteryear"s Food & Spirits. 200 S. Talbot Street. 410-745-6206
Carpenter Street Saloon. Talbot Street. 410-745-5111. The tavern was built in 1874, and has served as a bank, newspaper office, post office, and telephone company.
Jon and Mike's. 125 Mulberry Street. Opened 1998
Chesapeake Landing. Rte. 33. 410-745-9600

Favorite Candy Store:
St. Michael's Candy Company. 216 S. Talbot Street. 410-745-6060

Special Events:
Log Canoe Racing. Started in St. Michael's 1840-60 on Miles River and now being raced again in canoes many over a 100 years old. The canoes were once used to gather food, harvest shellfish and for transportation by the Indians. They are now a sight to behold. Races are held throughout the summer.
Wooden Boat Show. June
Classic and Antique Boat Show. June

Pot Pie

Pot Pie sterned boats were originally built on Harris' Creek.

Bozman

The town is named for the Bozman family. John Leeds Bozman wrote one of the early histories of Maryland.

Tilghman Island

Tilghman is an out of the way, but a lovely true Eastern Shore setting, where many of the families have lived in the same houses for generations. Separated from the Eastern Shore by the Knapps Narrows, it was once called Choptank Island. Tilghman was first charted by John Smith in 1608. The island was first surveyed for Seth foster in 1659. The island then passed to the Wardes, and later the Tilghman family. It was named for Matthew Tilghman who owned it in 1775 and was known as the "Patriarch of Maryland".

Tilghman Island was one of the main places for oystering on the Chesapeake. In 1897 the Tilghman Packing plant opened (until 1977). The skipjack became the most successful boat for dredging oysters.

The bridge across the Narrows was the longest single span drawbridge in Maryland and was built in 1934 (now at Chesapeake Maritime Museum in St. Michael's). A new bridge was built to replace it in 1998.

Tilghman Island is home to some of the last skipjacks (oystering boats) on the Chesapeake. The H.M. Krentz, owned by Ed Farley and the Rebecca T. Ruark, owned by Capt. Wade H. Murphy, Jr. still dredge oysters, and during the off-oyster season takes passengers for trips around the Bay.

Restaurants and Inns:
Pescado's. Rte. 33 and Knapps Narrows. 410-886-2126
Harrison's Chesapeake House. Rte 33. 410-886-2121
The Tilghman Island Inn. Coopertown Road. 410-886-2141. Recently renovated
Black Walnut Inn. Black Walnut Road. 410-886-2053
The Osprey. Knapps Narrows. 410-886-2330
Sinclair House. 5718 Black Walnut Point Road. 410-886-2147

Cambridge

The town was founded in 1684 as port of entry by the General Assembly, and incorporated 1794 on the Choptank River, part of the Choptank Indian Reservation. The Choptank River is the longest river on the Eastern Shore and is navigatable for 53 miles. Cambridge is the county seat for Dorchester County

This is the only deepwater port on the Eastern Shore. During the Revolutionary War Cambridge was the center for military operations on the Eastern Shore. During the mid 1800s large lumber and flour mills were located on Cambridge Creek. From here tobacco, muskrat pelts, and other products of the area, especially oysters during the 19th c were shipped. Timber was supplied to the Central Pacific railroad for building rail cars. Later shipbuilding became prominent, mainly for the Chesapeake Bay trade.

In the late 1800s Col. James Wallace began packing oysters, and Cambridge was second to Baltimore in the number of oysters shucked per year. The refrigerated rail car improved transport of the oysters, In 1911 Wallace's processing plant was sold to the Phillips Packing company. The company left the area in the 1950's. In 1910 a fire swept through Race and Muir Streets, burning many of the buildings.

Unfortunately in 1963 and 1967 the town had serious racial problems, and the Pine Street Elementary School was burned.

Attractions:
Christ Episcopal Church. Church founded 1693, present building dates from 1883. Five former Maryland governors are buried here.
Meredith House and Dorchester County Historical Society. Maryland Avenue. 410-228-7953. Built 1760. Georgian home
Neild Museum.902 LaGrange Avenue. 410-228-7953. Herb garden, smokehouse, Indian and agricultural artifacts
Brannock Maritime Museum. 210 Talbot Avenue. Great photographs and nautical artifacts
Richardson Museum. 401 High Street. The museum is named for James Richardson, an Eastern Shore shipbuilder. His boat, Mr. Jim, can be seen at the Chesapeake Bay Museum at St. Michael's. He built a replica of "The Dove", one of the original ships to sail to St. Mary's City.
Old Trinity Church. Near Cambridge on rte.16. Claims to be oldest Episcopal church in continuous use in U.S. and was built 1695.
Annie Oakley lived in Cambridge with her husband Frank Butler in a house built in 1912 at 28 Bellevue Avenue. She was a famous rifle woman and shot her first gun at age 9.
Birthplace of Harriet Tubman. Green Briar Road. 410-228-0401. Harriet Tubman was often called "the Moses of her People" when she worked for the Underground Railroad and helped free 300 slaves, of which she had been one.
100 High Street. The house was built in 1903 by Ellen S. Goldsborough, wife of Gov. Phillips Lee Goldsborough. A later owner was Gov. Emerson C. Harrington.
Many of the houses along High Street were built for members of the Goldsborough family. 200 High Street was built in 1790 for Charles Goldsborough. He became a US Congressman in 1805, and was the last Federalist Governor in Maryland, elected 1819.
Dorchester County Courthouse. 206 High Street. The building was built in 1854 and designed by Richard Upjohn, the architect of Trinity Church, New York.
Bayly House. 207 High Street. This house was built in Annapolis in 1755 and moved across the Bay in 1760 by John Caille.

Along Mill Street were built many homes for the Phillips family, of the Phillips Packing Company. Captain Levi Phillips, the founder of the company built the large house at 312 Mill Street.

701 Locust Street. Home built for Judge Henry Lloyd, later Governor of Maryland.

Sycamore Cottage. 417 High Street. Built after 1759 by Rev. Daniel Maynadier, a French Huguenot. Now home of the Cambridge Women's Club.

Piney Point on Phillips Creek. The plantation was purchased in 1690, and the house completed in 1710.

About six miles west of Cambridge on Rte. 343 is the Spocot Windmill, a reproduction of a "post mill".

On Bucktown Road is located the Brooks Barrel Company, the only remaining slack cooperage in Maryland.

Just south of Cambridge is Big Blackwater National Wildlife Refuge, located on Slaughter Creek.

Lodging:
Glasgow Inn. 1500 Hambrooks Boulevard. 410-228-0575. Ancestral home of Tubman family. Purchased by Dr. Robert F. Tubman in 1842. Originally land purchased by William Murray Ward in 1760 and house built that year. William Van Murray was Minister to Holland in 1800, and negotiated the Louisiana Purchase with France. Also served in U.S. Congress.
Cambridge House. 112 High Street. 410-221-7700. Former captain's mansion
Lodgecliffe on the Choptank. 103 Choptank Terrace. 410-228-1760

Restaurants:
The Blue Crab Restaurant on the Water. 203 Trenton Street 410-228-8877
High Spot Restaurant. 303 High Street. 410-228-3410
Snapper's Waterfront Café. 112 Commerce Street. 410-228-0112. Now home to the Lady Katie, one of the few skipjacks still oystering on the Chesapeake. The author's husband spent time aboard her when she was owned by Capt. Stanley Larrimore of Tilghman Island.
McGuigan's Pub and Restaurant. 411 Muse Street. 410-228-7110
Spicer's Seafood. Rte. 50 and Woods Road. 410-221-0222

Brewery:
Wild Goose Brewery. 20 Washington Street. 410-221-1122. Micro-brewery makes Wild Goose Amber.

Church Creek

Old Trinity Church. Rte.16. This is the oldest church in the United States still in use and built in 1675. The church is very small, only twenty feet by thirty-eight feet.

Choptank

Boats used to sail three times daily between here (once called Medford's Wharf) and Baltimore.

Sewall

Sewall was named for Henry Sewall, secretary of the province of Maryland under Charles Calvert, the third Lord Baltimore.

Golden Hill

St. Mary's Star of the Sea Church. Rte. 335. This small Roman Catholic church was built by Rev. Joseph Mosley, a Jesuit missionary, in 1769.

Vienna

Vienna is one of the oldest settlements on the Eastern Shore, dating back to 1669, and was once called Emperors Landing, or the "Town on the Nanticoke", as it is located on the Nanticoke River. The Colonial Assembly recommended the point as a ferry location in 1671. Vienna was founded by a decree of the Colonial Assembly in 1706. Jacob Lockerman was appointed to lay out the town. He suggested naming it for Vienna, Austria. It may also have been named for Vinnacokasimmon, an Indian chief. In 1768 it became the Custom's District for the region, and the original Custom's House still stands. Shipbuilding and cotton were important trades.

During the American Revolutionary War goods and supplies were shipped from here to the Continental Army. During the War of 1812 the British came up the Nanticoke River. Thomas Holiday Hicks, governor of Maryland during the Civil War lived here from 1829-40.

Attractions:
Governor Thomas Holiday Hicks House. Water Street. Home of governor who prevented Maryland from seceding during Civil War.
The Customs House. Church and Water Streets. Dates from 1768.

Lodging:
Tavern House B&B. 111 Water Street. C1800
Nanticoke Manor House. Church Street
Governor's Ordinary. Water & Church Streets

Salisbury

Salisbury was founded in 1732 and incorporated in 1811. It is located on the Wicomico River and is the largest city on the Eastern Shore. Most of the city was destroyed by fires in 1869 and 1886. Salisbury is the location of the Perdue Chicken headquarters. US Senator Paul Sarbanes was born in Salisbury, and actor John Glover grew up here. The National Indoor Tennis Championships were once held at the Civic Center which burned down.

Attractions:
Pemberton Hall and Wicomico Heritage Centre. Pemberton Drive. Built 1741 for Col. Isaac Handy owner of plantation and ships.
Mason-Dixon Line Marker. MD Rte. 467. Has coat of arms of George Washington and Lord Baltimore
Ward Museum of Waterfowl Art. 909 Shumaker Drive. 410-742-4988. Wonderful collection of decoys. Collection of master decoy carvers Lemuel and Steven Ward.
Poplar Hill Mansion. 117 Elizabeth Street. Built 1795 by Major Levin Handy, an officer in the Revolution.
Chipman Cultural Center. Broad and Ellen Streets. This building is used for various town cultural functions. It was originally the A.M.E Church, the oldest black church on the Eastern Shore. The land was purchased by 3 freemen in 1837 and part of the church built in 1838. Mr. and Mrs. Charles P. Chipman purchased the building, and gave the building to the Chipman Foundation. Mr. Chipman was Principal of the Colored Industrial High School, and later Salisbury High School.
The Salisbury Times is on the site of Camp Upton, a Civil War camp.
Ellis Bay Wildlife Management Area. 1,924 preserve.
Green Hill Church. Rte. 352 (12 miles outside town). Church built 1733, has oldest graveyard in U.S. Open by appointment
Salisbury Pewter. Rte. 13 North. Tours and pewter for sale
Salisbury Zoo and Park. 750 South Park Drive

Restaurants
Basil. 1137 S. Division Street. 410-548-2660

WhiteHaven

Whitehaven was once noted as a port, for shipbuilding and during the 1920's for rum running.

Attractions:
Old Green Hill Church. On Rte. 352. This church on the Wicomico River was built in 1733.

Hebron

Chesapeake Fire Museum. Rte. 670.

Princess Anne

Princess Anne was created by an Act of the Maryland General Assembly in 1733 and became a port on the Manokin River. Twenty-five acres of "Beckford", a plantation owned by David Brown, were purchased and divided into thirty equal lots with Bridge Street as the main street. The town was named in honor of King George II's daughter. The University of Maryland Eastern Shore was founded here in 1886 by the Delaware Conference of the Methodist Church to educate young black men and women. The town has many lovely buildings and time should be taken for a good walking tour.

Attractions:
Teackle Mansion.11736 Mansion Street. Beautiful neoclassical home built 1802-19. Home of Dennis Teackle, merchant and statesman, associate of Thomas Jefferson's. The house was the setting for "The Entailed Hat", a novel published in 1884 by George Alfred Townsend.
William Geddes House. Broad and Church Streets. Built c 1755 is the oldest dwelling in Queen Anne's.
Charles Jones House. Somerset Avenue. Built 1780 and is located on Lot 3, of the original 30 lots.
Woolford-Elzy House. Somerset Avenue. C 1788
Nutter's Purchase. Flurer'sLane. C 1800 as part of a tannery.
Linden Hill. Somerset Avenue. C 1835. Lovely Greek Revival home.

John W. Crisfield House. 30556 Somerset Avenue. C 1852 built by US Senator John Crisfield.

Beckford. C 1803 built by John Dennis, former US Senator.

St. Andrews Church built about 1770

Lodging:
The Washington Hotel and Inn. 11784 Somerset Avenue. 410-651-2525. An ordinary (hotel) has operated on this property since 1797.
Hayman House Bed and Breakfast. 30491 Prince William Street. 410-651-1107
Waterloo Country Inn. 28822 Mt. Vernon Road. 410-651-0883

Seward

Harriet Tubman Birthplace. Brodess Plantation. Mrs. Tubman was the founder of Underground Railroad during the Civil War and was known as the "Moses of her People".

Denton

Denton is located on the Choptank River and was the birthplace of Gov. Harry Hughes.

Attractions:
Caroline County Museum of Rural Life. On Court House Green. The Annie Taylor House was built c 1795.

Nassawango Iron Furnace

Attractions:
Furnace Town. Dates from 1840's. Village on 22 acres. 16 miles south of Salisbury on Old Furnace Road. One of the oldest hot-blast furnaces still intact. Restored 1966.

Snow Hill

Snow Hill was settled in 1642 by colonists from the "Snow Hill" section of London on the banks of the Pocomoke River. The town received its charter in 1686 and was made a Royal Port in 1694. The first Presbyterian Church in America was founded in Snow Hill in 1684. In 1742 it became the county seat of Worcester County. In 1793 the town was platted into 100 lots. As a port it served the western shore and was on the route to the Nassawango Iron Furnace which produced bog iron. The town has many lovely homes dating prior to 1877 and a walking tour is recommended (Maps available).

As many of the local shops closed, local merchants rallied to find alternative uses for them. Snow Hill is now billed as "The Antiques Capital of the Eastern Shore".

Attractions:
Worcester County Courthouse. The first was built 1742, burned 1834, and the present one in 1894. Market Street
The Julia A. Purnell Museum. 208 W. Market Street
All Hallows Episcopal Church. Market Street. Established 1692, present structure 1756. The bell was a gift from Queen Anne.
Mount Zion One-Room Schoolhouse Museum. Ironshire Street
Makemie Memorial Presbyterian Church. Built 1890, but the congregation was first organized in 1684.

Inns and B&B's:
Chanceford Hall Inn. 410-632-2231
Snow Hill Inn B&B. 410-632-2102
River House Inn. 410-632-2722

Berlin

Berlin was founded in the 1790's on a 300 acre grant to Burley Plantation in 1677. Commodore Stephen Decatur was born here in 1779. The town was incorporated in 1868. Berlin has 47 structures listed in the National Register of Historic Places.

Attractions:
Calvin B. Taylor House Museum. 208 North Main Street. Built 1832
Whaley House. 100 West Street. Earliest documented dwelling in Berlin, c 1800
Stevenson-Chandler House. 125 North Main Street. Dates from 1790's.
Kenwood. 101 South Main Street. Fine Federal woodwork
Telescopic House. 413 South main Street. Name from smaller wing next to larger one.
Waverly. 509 South Main. Federal style house
Pitts-Bounds House. 23 South Main Street. Wrap-around verandah, built 1890's on site of Burley Inn

Lodging:
Merry Sherwood Plantation. 8909 Worchester Highway. 410-641-2112.
Magnificent pre-Civil War Mansion.
Atlantic Hotel. 2 North Main Street. 410-641-3589. On National Register of
Historic Places

Crisfield

Far down the Eastern Shore is Crisfield, still home to many watermen. The town was originally named Annemessex, the Algonquin name meaning "Bountiful Waters". The town was first surveyed in 1663. This was an agricultural area and then fishing became important. The town was renamed Somers Cove, and later named for John Woodland Crisfield (1808-97), a former congressman, who financed the Eastern Shore Railroad. Seafood could now be transported more quickly. Crisfield was then called "Seafood Capital of the World". Isaac Solomon who had patented a pasturizing canning process, brought his ideas to Crisfield and set up a processing plant here. By 1910 the Crisfield Customs House had the largest registry of sailing vessels in the U.S.

Sadly most of the canning and processing facilities are closed down. The town has experienced some lean times, and now depends on seafood festivals and other promotions.

Attractions:
Makepeace. Built 1663
Crockett House. Main Street. 1888. Historic Victorian
Ward Brothers' Home. Home of Lem and Steve Ward - famous for making decoys.
Tawes Museum. Somers Cove Marina. Honors Gov. J. Millard Tawes (1894-1979) who was a native of Crisfield.
Rhehobeth Presbyterian Church. Rte. 406 outside Crisfield. The church is the oldest Presbyterian church in the United States, built in 1706 by Reverend Francis Makemis, "Father of the American Presbyterian Church.

Restaurants
Captain's Galley. W. Main Street. 410-968-1636
Waterman's Inn. 410-968-2119
Side Street Seafood Market & Restaurant. 410-968-2442

Special Events:
Crab and Clam Bake - third Wednesday in July
Crab Derby - Labor Day week-end

Smith Island

Smith Island was visited by and named for Capt. John Smith who explored the Chesapeake in 1608. The island was settled in the17[th] c by farmers. Over 50 skipjacks once operated from here. Watermen still provide the bounty of the Chesapeake to a co-op for crab that runs May to October. After picking these crabs are sent to Crisfield by boat.

Smith Island can be reached by ferry from Crisfield. The island has lost over 1200 acres to the Bay, but three main communities are located here. The land was used mainly for raising sheep and cattle. Later the island became known for its seafood. Many of the same families are still here, often speaking a dialect that even "mainlanders' have trouble understanding. The island's religious roots revolve around the Methodist faith, and "camp meetings" are a yearly event.

Lodging:
Inn of Silent Music. Tylertown. 410-425-3541
Ewell Tide Inn. 410-425-2141
Smith island Motel. Ewell. 410-425-3321

Dining:
Rukes. 410-425-2311
Bayside Inn. Ewell. 410-425-2771
Inn of Silent Music. 410-425-3541

Tangier Island

Tangier Island was also visited by Capt. John Smith in 1608. The island was an operating base for the British during the War of 1812. The dialect is native to here, and sometimes can be difficult to understand.

Blackwater National Wildlife Refuge

Off Route 16. Tours, trails, biking. Rare birds, animals, marshes. Nearby are Hooper's Island, Taylor's Island, and Barren Island.

East New Market

East New Market was settled in the mid 17th c as a village and site of a fort. The first white settler was thought to be John Edmonston who came from Virginia in the 1660's to seek religious freedom. He was later joined by Col. James O'Sullivane. The original name of the town was "Crossroads". The New Market Academy was founded in 1818. It has been an agricultural center for three centuries, and in 1975 became a Historic District and was entered in the National Register of Historic Places.

Attractions:

Friendship Hall. Built 1740's and later home of Col. James O'Sullivane.

Buckland. Home built for Dr. Daniel O'Sullivane. Once known as Maurice Hall.

Edmonston House. C 1780-90 probably by O'Sullivane family. The Edmonston family bought the property known as "Liberty Hall" in 1840.

Little Manning House. C 18th c. This is located on property originally part of the Nanticoke Manor Tract c 1600.

Smith Cottage. Built 1760 probably by O'Sullivane family.

House of the Hinges. c 1750 built by the Ennalls family. Lovely Federal home. It was later owned by Major Anthony Manning, a member of the Maryland Cavalry during the War of 1812, and later by his son, Dr. Anthony Manning, a Union surgeon during the Civil War. The name comes from the log building located behind the house, which has large hinges on the doors.

New Market House. c1780. The town was named for the house which sat on a tract of 7 seven acres. James O'Sullivane sold the property in 1787 to James Daffin, and it was sold again in 1790 to George Goodwin.

Deal Island

The island was first called Devil's Island by the survivors of a 17th c shipwreck. Later home to Joshua Thomas, "Parson of the Islands" who established many Methodist churches in the area. Crabbing and Oystering are very important, and Deal is said to have the largest number of skipjacks still around.

Bloodworth Island

Near Deal. The island has used by the Navy for target practice since 1942. In 1997 nesting osprey forced the cancellation of this practice.

Parson Island

Parson Island was named for Joshua Thomas "Parson of the Islands". It was bought by McCormick and Co. in 1944 for a spice experimentation and conference center.

Poplar Islands

The islands are off Tilghman and are made up of Poplar, Jefferson and Coach Islands. The first settlers, Richard Thompson and his family were killed by the Indians. In 1847 Charles Carroll the grandson of Charles Carroll of Carrollton raised black cats here to send pelts to China. A long cold winter caused the ice to freeze and a natural bridge allowed the cats to escape to the mainland.

Still Pond

Still Pond was originally named Steele's Pone, "Steels Favorite", from Elizabethan English. In 1841 Tom Hyer who lived here won the first American heavyweight boxing championship, beating Yankee Sullivan. This was the first place to grant women's suffrage in Maryland in 1908.

Near here on Coopers Lane is Drayton Manor, once a large estate and now a Methodist Retreat.

Locust Grove

Shrewsbury Church. Rte. 213N. Built 1832. Many veterans buried here, including Brig. Gen. John Cadwalder, Revolutionary soldier. The parish was originally established on the Sassafras River in 1692.

Cecilton

Attractions:
St. Steven's Episcopal Church. Rte. 282. The Sassafras Parish was established in 1692. The bell was presented by Queen Anne.
St. Francis Xavier Roman Catholic Church (Old Bohemia Mission). Bohemia Church Road. Charles Carroll, a Signer of the Declaration of Independence and his brother John, the first Catholic Bishop in the United States and founder of

Georgetown University, attended the Old Bohemia Mission, which was established in 1745. Kitty Knight is buried in the cemetery.

Chesapeake City

Chesapeake City is located on the C&D Canal that connects the Delaware River and the Chesapeake Bay, and was officially opened on July 4, 1829, at the most northern end of the Eastern Shore. This picturesque town has some lovely shops, inns and restaurants along the canal. The canal was purchased by the U.S. government in 1919 and has been widened and improved several times. The town was once known as "The Village of Bohemia".

Attractions:
Chesapeake & Delaware Canal Museum. 410-885-5621
Captain Layman House. Built c 1830 for proprietor of Bayard House

Hotels/Inns:
Inn at the Canal. 104 Bohemia Avenue. 410-885-5995
The Blue Max Inn. 300 Bohemia Avenue. 410-885-2781. The William Lindsey House. Built c 1854. Once owned by Jack Hunter who wrote "The Blue Max". Shipwatch Inn. 401 First Street. 410-885-5300
Bohemia Manor. 1236 Town Point Road. 410-885-3024. Victorian B&B

Restaurants:
Bayard House. 11 Bohemia Avenue. 410-885-5040. First place with vegetable crab soup category at the Maryland Seafood Festival. Building dates c 1780
Chesapeake Inn. C&D Canal. 410-885-2040
Canal Creamery. 9 Bohemia Avenue. Ice cream parlor
The Tap Room. Corner of 2nd and Bohemia. 410-885-9873. Seafood
Village Café. 401 Second Street. 410-885-2294
Bakers Restaurant. 1075 Augustine Herman Highway. 410-398-2435

Special Meeting Facilities

The Aspen Institute. Wye River Conference Center. 201 Wye Woods Way. Queenstown. 410-827-7400
The Tidewater Inn & Conference Center. 101 East Dover Street. Easton. 410-822-1300

Did You Know?

Queen Anne County was named for her "gracious majesty" Queen Anne, daughter of King George II of England.

Somerset County is named for Mary Somerset, sister-in-law of Cecil Calvert, the 2nd Lord Baltimore. Established 1666.

Talbot County was first settled in the 1650's, mainly by Quakers, and Puritans from Virginia. The county is named for Lady Grace Talbot, sister of the second Lord Baltimore.

The Sassafras River was discovered by Captain John Smith and is named for the Indians who lived here.

Dorchester County was originally called Dorset in honor of the 4th Earl of Dorset., and became a politcal entity in 1669.
Kent County was first explored by Captain John Smith in 1608. Kent County was founded in 1642 and named for Kent, England from which many of the earliest colonists had come. The first legislature convened in 1649. The first settlement was New Yarmouth, but in 1706 with the founding of Chestertown, this now became the economic center and port.

The Mason-Dixon Line is a 233 mile line surveyed 1763-67 by the English surveyors Charles Mason and Jeremiah Dixon to settle a boundary dispute between the Calvert and Penn families, proprietors of Maryland and Pennsylvania respectively.. Stones are placed every mile. Every fifth marker is a "crownstone" bearing the arms of the Calverts on one side and the Penns on the other. The first of these stones is on State Route 54. The Mason-Dixon Line was to play an important role in the Civil War by dividing North and South.

The area north of the Choptank River, covering Tilghman's Island, Tilghman's Neck, and the Poplar Islands, is called Bay Hundred. The name comes from the early division of Maryland into "hundreds". This is a term that dates from the Anglo-Saxon period in England, where an English "Hundred" contained ten families, ten estates of fighting men.

Chapter 13

Annapolis, Chesapeake Bay and Naval Academy Books

Annapolis, A Walk Through History   Elizabeth B. Anderson

Annapolis Houses 1700-75   Deering Davis

Annapolis   Kevin Fleming

Annapolis, A Portrait   Ron Pilling

The State House at Annapolis   Morris L. Radoff

"The Train's Been Done and Gone"   Marion E. Warren and Mame Warren

Then Again...Annapolis   Mame Warren

The Chesapeake Bay Book   Allison Blake

Chesapeake Bay Walk   Dave Bell

Tidewater Triumph   Geoffrey M. Footner

William Paca   Stiverson E. Jacobsen

Annapolis   William Martin

Annapolis Maryland Families   Robert H. McIntire

Watermen   Randall Peffer

This was Chesapeake Bay   Robert H. Burgess

Chesapeake Circle   Robert H. Burgess

Bay Ridge on the Chesapeake   Jane Wilson McWilliams and Carol Cushard Patterson

Annapolis Today   Kendall Banning

Bay Beacons, Lighthouses of the Chesapeake Bay   Linda Turbyville

Trumpy   Robert Tolf

Chesapeake   James Michener

Cruising the Chesapeake   William H. Shellenberger

Chesapeake Country   Eugene L. Meyer

A Century of "Separate But Equal" Education in Anne Arundel County and

The Other Annapolis 1900-1950   Philip L. Brown

St. Anne's Annapolis History and Times   William K. Paynter

Buildings of the State of Maryland at Annapolis   Morris L. Radoff

The Quays of the City   Shirley V. Baltz

Yesteryear in Annapolis   Harold N. Burdett

Compass Pointers and other Streets of Annapolis   George and Virginia Shaun

Antiques in Annapolis   Wendell Garrett

Colonial Annapolis   Historic Annapolis Foundation

Builders of Annapolis   Norman K. Risjord

Annapolis Today   Kenneth Banning

Dr. Richard Hill of London Town: Economic and Social Perspectives on Life in
Colonial America   Mechelle Kearns

Tyde 'n Thyme   Junior League of Annapolis

Angel Food   St. Anne's Church

Maryland's Way   Hammond-Harwood House Cookbook

Chesapeake Bay Cooking   John Shields

Chesapeake Bay Crab Cookbook   John Shields

Maryland Seafood Cookbook I, II, III   Maryland Dept. of Agriculture

Flavor of the Chesapeake Bay Cookbook   Whitey Schmidt

The Crab Cookbook   Whitey Schmidt

The Official Crab Eater's Guide   Whitey Schmidt

A Guide to Chesapeake Seafood Dining-Bayside Views to Dine By   Whitey Schmidt

Tidewater on the Halfshell   The Junior League of Norfolk-Virginia Beach

My Favorite Recipes   Helen Avalynne Tawes

Sailing at the Naval Academy   Adm. Robert McNitt '38

Thunder Below   Adm.Eugene Fluckey '35

The U.S. Naval Academy   Jack Sweetman

A Day in the life of Midshipman   Sandra Travis-Bidahl

The Brigade in Review   Robert Stewart

Brigade, Seats. The Naval Academy Cokkbook   Karen Gibson

Service Etiquette   Oretha D. Schwartz

The Naval Academy Candidate Book; Reef Points; and the Plebes Bible
William L. Smallwood

About the Author and Illustrator, and Family

Katie Barney Moose, born in Baltimore, is a descendant of the Clagett family of Maryland, and many old New England whaling families. Born a Barney she has been unable to trace her lineage to Captain Joshua Barney, the famous Naval hero of the War of 1812.

She has lived in many of the U.S.' great architectural, historical and waterside gems besides Annapolis - New Castle, DE; Newport and Providence, RI; Cold Spring Harbor, NY; San Francisco; Philadelphia; Greenwich, CT; Alexandria, VA; Washington, DC; and New York City. She and her family also maintain homes on historic Nantucket Island.

Mrs. Moose is the co-author of "The Best of Newport, the Newport Guidebook", several publications on the fiber optic telecommunications business, and is a consultant on international business and protocol. Her hobbies include gourmet cooking, fine wines, history, sailing, genealogy, theology and travel.

Ginger Doyel, the illustrator, is a fourth generation Annapolitan. She attended the Severn School, and graduated from St. Mary's High School. She studied landscape architecture at the University of Maryland, and is a member of the class of 2001 at the University of Richmond.

Miss Doyel's interests include travel, painting, golf, sailing and flying. She has lived in several states and countries, but calls Annapolis home.

George Moose, though raised in North Carolina has spent much time living on the Eastern Shore and twice in Annapolis. His love for the sea stems from the time he spent with Capt. Stanley Larrimore aboard the skipjack, the Lady Katie, now in Cambridge. His work at Fawcett Boat Supplies in Annapolis has brought him in touch with many of yachting's finest.

Mr. Moose has also learned to restore fine antiques, and with a degree in history, appreciates the significance of Annapolis' history. He is an excellent sailor, gourmet chef, genealogist, and avid reader.

Order Form

To order extra copies of "Annapolis: The Guidebook", please fill out this form:

Name_____

Address_____

_____

Telephone_____

Please send _____ copies of Annapolis: The Guidebook @ $13.95 each

Postage @ $2.50 per copy

Total_____

Send To:

Conduit Press
111 Conduit Street
Annapolis, MD 21401

For further information please
- call 410-280-5272
- Fax 410-263-5380
- E-mail: kaholmes@erols.com

Notes